THE LION

THE LAMB

Reflections on the Book of Revelation

VOLUME ONE

THE LION

&

THE LAMB

Reflections on the Book of Revelation

VOLUME ONE

TONY LING

DESTINY IMAGE EUROPE™ **srl**
Via Maiella, 1
66020 San Giovanni Teatino (Ch) - Italy

"Changing the world, one book at a time."

This book and all other Destiny Image Europe™ books are available at Christian bookstores and distributors worldwide.

To order products, or for any other correspondence:

DESTINY IMAGE EUROPE™ **srl**
Via Acquacorrente, 6
65123 - Pescara - Italy
Tel. +39 085 4716623 - Fax: +39 085 4716622
E-mail: info@eurodestinyimage.com

Or reach us on the Internet: **www.eurodestinyimage.com**

Cover Design by Debbie Swift/Entheos Design
Cover Photo by Shelly Snyder/Snyder Studio

ISBN 10: 88-89127-39-2
ISBN 13: 978 88-89127-39-1

For Worldwide Distribution, Printed in Italy.

1 2 3 4 5 6 7 8/10 09 08 07 06

Dedication

To Keri Jones, Noralv Askeland, and Chandrakant Chavada, "…outstanding among the apostles."

In loving memory of Hazel, 1943–2002, "prepared as a bride…for her husband."

Acknowledgments

Encouragement and support for this book has come from many friends and colleagues around the world. Thank you, brothers.

Those closer to home have provided much needed practical help and support. For transcribing the original messages and helping to work them into readable manuscripts, I give grateful thanks to Heather Cursham, Kim Murden, Sara Cosgrove, and Jacqueline Hamer-Hodges.

My thanks to Ron Eagle and Matthew Ling, who ministered with me in the conference from which these words are taken. Their valuable contributions are not in this book, but they can be obtained in audio format from the School of the Prophets.

To Geoff and Pam Grice and Dave and Su Gregg, part of the leadership team at Southport Community Church, I am indebted to you and appreciate you all.

The highest appreciation to my friend and fellow minister Trevor Lloyd, leading elder at Community Church, Huddersfield. Thanks, Trev, for all your hard work, encouragement, faithfulness—and occasional nagging. We got there in the end!

Endorsements

Tony Ling is an author you can trust. He takes the Book of Revelation out of the hands of weird end-time theorists and gives it back to the people of God as a word from the Lord to strengthen and encourage them right now. He connects Revelation to the whole of Scripture and shows that Jesus is at the center of its message. This book is not just for those particularly interested in Revelation, but for everyone who wants to grow in their faith.

Timothy Larsen, PhD
Professor of Theology
Wheaton College Wheaton, Illinois

Tony Ling opens up the Book of Revelation, changing it from something complicated and distant into a focused, helpful, and Jesus-centered Scripture.

Through his profound knowledge of the Word of God, he shows us that the Book of Revelation is, as it says in the first verse, "The revelation of Jesus Christ...." Jesus is the center, not only of the Church, but of the whole universe. The Revelation makes us see Him as the one who leads His people through to victory through all times.

The perspectives in this book inspire us to fulfill our Kingdom destiny here on Earth.

From my point of view, Tony Ling is the best person to write a book on this subject. Thank God he did it! I gladly recommend this book.

Morten Askeland
Leading Pastor, Christian Fellowship, Bergen
Principal, Bergen Bible School

In *The Lion and the Lamb,* Tony Ling has drawn on his vast knowledge of the great themes of Scripture to produce a thorough biblical exposition of the climax of God's Word. That is the beauty of this book: the author has broken out of the narrow confines of other lines of thought to place John's letter to the seven churches within the wider framework of the other sixty-five books in the Bible. And he achieves it in a style that is easy to read.

This is not just a book for those who want to know what Revelation is all about; it's for those who want to know what the Bible is all about.

Dr. Roger Aubrey
Principal
Covenant School of Ministries, School of the Word

Contents

Foreword

Over the past two millennia, Revelation has evoked many different responses: faith, doubt, joy, dismay, triumph, anticipation—and certainly bewilderment and confusion. Some love to dwell in its pages (it was always my father's favorite book of the Bible), but others virtually ignore it, wanting to avoid the errors of those whose interpretations and applications did not stand the test of time.

Having personally read through the Book of Revelation many times, studied related books and commentaries, and preached through much of the text, I have over time come to the same eschatological position as the author's. But that is not to say you must agree with a particular position in order to benefit from this book. I found within these pages at least four powerful "revelations" that go beyond doctrinal position: revelations that capture your attention and your heart and, if embraced, will transform your life and ministry.

First, Tony Ling makes absolutely certain that the center—the "jewel in the crown"—is always Christ Jesus. It's all about Him! A few years ago at a Christian conference attended by some 17,000 delegates, I was greatly saddened to observe that in a five-day period only one speaker focused on lifting up the name of Jesus. In Christian bookstores we find innumerable books and magazines that are all about achieving success by simply following the methods and models used by the author. This book has nothing to say about methodology; it has everything to say about Christ.

The second key theme or revelation is one that would save many pastors and leaders from handling the message of God's victorious Kingdom in a triumphalistic manner. It is that the Lion of Judah is also the Sacrificial Lamb—all-powerful and all-knowing, yet meek and humble of heart. How I wish this book had been available fifty years earlier. So many young leaders in the charismatic movement of the twentieth century (myself included) acted like the rich man of Proverbs 18:23: "The poor man utters supplications, but the rich man answers roughly" (NASB).

A third revelation concerns the indispensable place of prayer, as portrayed by the altar of incense. When I read this section in the book, I felt as if I was standing on holy ground. Tony writes, "When our prayers touch the throne, the throne touches our world. The Kingdom comes on Earth when the church specifically prays for it to come."

A fourth major theme I found in *The Lion and the Lamb* was that the Old Testament and New Testament are inseparably joined; Scripture portrays an unfolding of God's covenants from Genesis to Revelation. Tony obviously loves God's Word and (from my observation) loves truth regardless of the cost. He doesn't shrink back from speaking what's in his heart—and in so doing may offend some of our cherished beliefs or pet interpretations. If or when that occurs, I would simply encourage the reader to ask, does this measure up with Scripture?

All in all, this book is a rich treasure chest. Throughout *The Lion and the Lamb* we are constantly offered nuggets of "prophetic gold." On almost every page I found myself underscoring something that grabbed my attention or making mental notes to look up some related Scripture. I pray that this book will be a great blessing to many.

Barnabas Coombs
Salt & Light Ministries
Church Relief International

Introduction

I love the Book of Revelation. I have preached from its treasury many times over many years. I have meditated on it often, and I have always been inspired by the deeply devotional passages with which it richly abounds.

I have studied numerous commentaries on Revelation—from the serious academic and theological to the desperately weird and flaky. I am aware of the various "millennial" positions held by different scholars and continue to be amazed at the ever-growing catalog of candidates for the role of "the beast."

But I am not a theologian, and this is not a commentary. This book is far from exhaustive in its treatment of John's magnificent prophecy, for the chapters herein were originally spoken messages delivered at a prophetic conference; they were designed to be practical and applicable.

I had previously taught the Book of Revelation to a Bible College class, and in the week that my wife died, we had been focused on the verse that says, "Blessed are those who die in the Lord from now on." Suddenly it was very real to me. Upon the foundation of this verse I experienced such comfort, encouragement, and strength through the Holy Spirit as is hard to explain to those who have never known it for themselves. Experientially, I understood that this was the very purpose of Revelation. But, of course, one cannot interpret Scripture by experience. Scripture must be interpreted by Scripture, and Scripture had already convinced me of the fact that Revelation was written not to predict some distant and obscure future but to encourage those who were living through (or immediately about to live through) the events portrayed with such drama, imagery, and prophetic poetry. But the first-century immediacy of Revelation in no way robs it of its potency or relevance—any more than Isaiah or Psalms have been rendered obsolete by the passage of time. It is the Word of God to every generation, profitable for teaching, rebuking, correcting, and training in righteousness; it is living and active.

At one time, John tells us, "I wept and wept." But his weeping was not for his own isolation or discomfort. He cries when it seems that the purposes of God have ground to a halt—for there is no one worthy to open the scroll. But "the Lion of Judah...has triumphed" (Rev. 5:5). Then, says John, "I saw a Lamb." John looks to see the triumphant Lion, only to discover a slain Lamb. The Lion-Lamb identity of Jesus is a seamless robe of inseparable character. Although throughout the book

18

John repeatedly identifies Jesus as the Lamb, it is always a Lamb of unconquerable strength, unmatchable power, and irresistible authority. The Lamb has a Lion's heart. The Lion of Judah has triumphed; he has the ability to open the scroll and set in motion all the purposes of God. But he triumphed in the laying down of his life, for the Lion has the nature of the sacrificial Lamb.

Revelation is full of enigmas, but none more profound than this—a Lion with the disposition of a Lamb; a Lamb with the characteristics of a Lion. It is only in Jesus that these extremes of character, both essential for redemption and rule, can live in perfect harmony. He is the Lion and the Lamb.

CHAPTER 1

It's All About Jesus

The Nature of Revelation

What kind of writing is the Book of Revelation? First of all, it is an *apocalypse.* The word apocalypse simply means an unveiling—taking the cover off. That should give us a clue that Revelation is not supposed to be confusing. It's not supposed to be frightening. Its meaning is not supposed to be up for grabs. It is meant to be the removing of a veil so that we can see clearly. And the first recipients of this book, the first-century church, would have understood it without recourse to the morning's newspaper. They would have understood it without studying the political situation around the world. Politics certainly comes into it, but it would have been relevant and meaningful to them in a way that it is not always to us.

Secondly, it is a *prophecy*. We are told this right at the beginning. We are to hear and respond to the words of this prophecy (Rev. 1:3). That makes it unique in the New Testament, for it is the only prophetic book found there. Most of the prophets we discover in the Old Testament. And yet in reading what those prophets wrote, we discover that they all prophesied about the days into which we have come. They prophesied about the Christ who was yet to be born (1 Pet. 1:10-12).

Because it is about the one to whom all the prophets pointed, this book is a not only an apocalypse, but more specifically a revelation of Jesus Christ (Rev. 1:1). It is not a revelation about the dragon, the beast, or the false prophet. It is a revelation of Jesus Christ. The book is all about Jesus. It is very important that we understand this. This book is not here to give us nightmares. It is here to give us comfort and hope, because it is all about Jesus.

Because it reveals Jesus to us, we can say that the Book of Revelation is also a very *devotional book.* Reading it should cause your heart to soar in thanksgiving to God. Reading the Book of Revelation should excite you because of the portrait that it paints of Jesus. Nowhere else in the New Testament will you find the dramatic and awesome pictures of Christ that are revealed to us in this book. Even the first chapter opens with a vision of Jesus that is heart warming, soul stirring, and awesome in its magnitude. There are other varied portraits of Christ that Revelation paints for us, and we will look at many of them in the course of this book. And as we look at them, they should cause our hearts to respond in adoration of Him; for, as we read the Book of Revelation, we discover again and again that the inhabitants of Heaven and the inhabitants of Earth are moved to worship Him who sits upon the throne and who lives forever and ever!

The Structure of Revelation

In terms of structure, we find that it is a book of *repetition* or *recapitulation*. Let me explain. You know what happens when you sit at home and watch the big game. You enjoy the action, get excited by the skill of the team you support, and are thrilled when they score. It is a tremendous moment of excitement and involvement. And then, when there is a particularly good moment, or a great score, there will be a replay, perhaps in slow motion. And then one of the announcers will say, "Let's look at that play from another angle." And so you often see the same goal played four or five times from different angles, with different views, from different perspectives. That is what the Book of Revelation is like. It repeats and recapitulates. It shows us something and then it is as if John says, "Let's look at that from another angle," and he goes back over the same ground and paints the picture from a different perspective. Sometimes you will see things that you did not see in the first account. That is the whole point of it. You will see things that were hidden from you in the first act, but when you see it repeated, you see it from a different angle and you get a fuller picture. That is what happens in the Book of Revelation. It does not progress chronologically. It is watching the same scene very often, from different angles.

Now this is a very important point if we are to understand the book correctly. And so for those of you who are not taken with sports and who are not interested in watching replays, let me put it in another way. Did you ever sit and watch a movie, and suddenly it goes blurry, or it wobbles, or it goes from color to black and white? And it's meant to happen—there's nothing wrong with the TV. It is the director's clue that you are watching a flashback. And the flashback is essential to the plot because you cannot under-stand what is going to happen next unless you see what happened before. It is a device that filmmakers use to keep the story flowing. Now, the apostle John does that. He takes us forward in the story line of Revelation, but then he will go back again and show us how we got there. He will show us the reason it all happened. He will give us the clue to the plot that is unfolding. As we go through this book, we will try to look and gather together some of those con-cepts and ideas that recur throughout Revelation.

What we have said about structure so far concerns the time ele-ment in Revelation. But its structure is also affected by place. As well as the interaction of different time dimensions, there are also two main places or backdrops against which the action of Revela-tion takes place. As you read the book you discover that there are *two main locations.* The first location is the *Heavenly temple.* All kinds of things are going on in Heaven. The second location is the *sinful world.* The Heavenly location is full of praise, worship, and adoration. The sinful world is full of rebellion, pestilence, and plague. But the whole purpose of Revelation is to bring Heaven down on the earth so that the peace and the blessings of Heaven might be seen and experienced in the world.

The Book of Revelation also has *two major motifs* that continually emerge. A motif is simply a recurring picture or image, a repeated metaphorical pattern or theme that the writer uses to convey something. The two motifs used in Revelation are the Old Testament events related to Egypt and Babylon. Both were places of captivity and oppression for God's people, and from both the Lord graciously delivered them. Egypt was the place of Israel's slavery, and Babylon came more and more to epitomize the dangers of captivating deception and so, in a sense, both continue as metaphoric pictures of those dangers. We will return to these in later chapters, but let us note here that there is more Old Testament in the Book of Revelation than probably anywhere else in the New Testament. It is packed with Old Testament illustrations and metaphor, Old Testament Scriptures, Old Testament events, Old Testament history. It is just full of the Old Testament. That is why it is very important for us as New Testament believers to be very familiar with the Old Testament Scriptures. We cannot ignore them. In fact, we ignore them at our peril, for ignoring what they say leads us into error in the New Testament. God does not have two different books. He has one book, and the two parts are inseparably joined together. The Old Testament prepares us for everything that is to come. The New Testament explains to us everything that has happened so far. I think it was Augustine who said, "The New is in the Old concealed, the Old is in the New revealed," and we will find it extremely difficult to come to terms with the Book of Revelation in any meaningful way if we are not familiar with Old Testament Scriptures. This is so important that we need to take time to look more closely at the Old Testament backdrop.

The Old Testament Background

One of the things we need to appreciate is that the New Testament Church was soaked in Old Testament Scripture. It was their missionary Bible. It was the only Bible they had. Paul can write to Timothy and say, "From infancy you have known the holy Scriptures, which are able to make you wise for salvation through faith in Christ Jesus" (2 Tim. 3:15). As far as Paul was concerned, you could get saved by faith in Christ through the Old Testament Scriptures. In fact, it tells us that Apollos proved from the Scriptures that Jesus was the Christ (Acts 18:28).

The whole of the New Testament finds its root and its inspiration in Old Testament Scriptures. Jesus himself made that very clear. He said to the Pharisees, "You diligently study the Scriptures because you think that by them you possess eternal life. These are the Scriptures that testify about Me" (John 5:39). Another time, on the Emmaus Road, when those two disciples are downcast because Jesus has been crucified, Jesus says, "'How foolish you are, and how slow of heart to believe all that the prophets have spoken! Did not the Christ have to suffer these things and then enter his glory?' And beginning with Moses and all the Prophets, He explained to them what was said in all the Scriptures concerning Himself" (Luke 24:25-27).

The prophets who prophesied of the coming salvation, Peter tells us, "searched intently and with the greatest care, trying to find out the time and circumstances to which the Spirit of Christ in them was pointing when He predicted the sufferings of Christ and the glories that would follow. It was revealed to them that they were not serving themselves but you, when they spoke of the things that have now been told you by those who have preached the Gospel to you by the Holy Spirit sent from heaven" (1 Pet. 1:10-12). They were speaking for a generation not yet born. They were speaking for a nation not yet on the earth. They were speaking for you and me. They were prophesying for us, because they were speaking about Jesus.

It's All About Jesus!

The great divide in peoples' understanding of Scriptures comes down to this. Is the Bible all about Israel, or is the Bible all about Jesus? That is the great divide. If it is all about Israel, I have nothing to say, but if it is all about Jesus, then I do not have enough space to say all that I need to say. My premise is that the Bible is all about Jesus. From Genesis to Revelation it is all about Jesus. Let me give you just one example for now. Do you remember when God brings Eve to Adam and Adam says, this is it, "For this reason a man will leave his father and mother and be united to his wife, and they will become one flesh" (Gen. 2:24)? Now that was true for Adam and Eve, but Jesus is the ultimate fulfillment even of that statement way back in Genesis. Paul takes it up in his letter to the Ephesians when he is exhorting husbands to love their wives and speaks of us being one with Him. He writes, "'For this reason a man will leave his father and mother and be united to his wife, and the two will become one flesh.' This is a profound mystery— but I am talking about Christ and the church" (Eph. 5:31-32). The whole of Scripture, from Genesis to Revelation, is about Jesus. God's purpose for His Son was that in all things He should have the preeminence, and all things includes the Bible. In the Word He should have preeminence, and in reading and studying and seeking to understand the Book of Revelation we want to give Jesus the preeminence. We want to be moved toward Christ again, to be touched by His love, stirred by His power, and inspired by His goodness. It is all about Jesus. We will have to touch on some things that are clearly anti-Christ, but we only touch on them to show that they pale into insignificance before Christ. They lose their horror, their darkness, and their fearsomeness in the light of Him who is truly King of kings and Lord of lords. This book is all about Jesus.

Revelation One

Let us start then by looking at part of chapter one that gives us one of those awesome portraits of Christ:

I, John, your brother and companion in the suffering and kingdom and patient endurance that are ours in Jesus, was on the island of Patmos because of the word of God and the testimony of Jesus. On the Lord's Day I was in the Spirit, and I heard behind me a loud voice like a trumpet, which said: "Write on a scroll what you see and send it to the seven churches: to Ephesus, Smyrna, Pergamum, Thyatira, Sardis, Philadelphia and Laodicea."

I turned around to see the voice that was speaking to me. And when I turned I saw seven golden lampstands, and among the lampstands was someone "like a son of man," dressed in a robe reaching down to his feet and with a golden sash around his chest. His head and hair were white like wool, as white as snow, and his eyes were like blazing fire. His feet were like bronze glowing in a furnace, and his voice was like the sound of rushing waters. In his right hand he held seven stars, and out of his mouth came a sharp double-edged sword. His face was like the sun shining in all its brilliance.

When I saw him, I fell at his feet as though dead. Then he placed his right hand on me and said: "Do not be afraid. I am the First and the Last. I am the Living One; I was dead, and behold I am alive for ever and ever! And I hold the keys of death and Hades.

"Write, therefore, what you have seen, what is now and what will take place later. The mystery of the seven stars that you saw in my right hand and of the seven golden lampstands is this: The seven stars are the angels of the seven churches, and the seven lampstands are the seven churches" (Revelation 1:9-20).

We only have to read this description and some of the interpretations of the vision that Jesus Himself gives to understand that the number seven is of special significance. The number seven of course represents fullness, or completeness. It is a number that will recur again and again through the Book of Revelation, in obvious statements like this but also in less obvious ways, and we will deal with that in more detail in a later chapter. For now, I want to focus on some of the descriptions of Jesus.

The Glowing Feet

I noted earlier that there are *two motifs* that dominate much of this book. They are two periods of Jewish history that form a kind of metaphorical basis or backdrop for the book: firstly, *Israel's slavery in Egypt* and secondly, *their bondage in Babylon.* We will find that the Egypt scene recurs again and again throughout the Scriptures, and we will look at this more closely in a chapter in Volume 2 called "The Exodus Paradigm" because there is so much of the Exodus that finds repetition in Revelation. Then, as you read through the Book of Revelation, you see that the great antagonist toward the people of God is revealed toward the end of the book as Babylon, the great prostitute.

Egypt and Babylon form part of the backdrop because, as people suffered under the taskmasters of Egypt, so people suffer today under the taskmasters of corrupt governments and anti-Christian philosophies. Just as people were carried away to Babylon, so people are carried away in the deceptions of the great prostitute who entices them away from their relationship with Jesus. These, therefore, are still relevant, and they were relevant in the first century when John wrote this letter from Jesus to His churches. He wrote to seven churches in Asia, although at this time there were more than seven churches. We will explore why it is seven churches a little later on.

One of the ways that periods of captivity for Israel were described is indicated by the words of Moses in Deuteronomy: "The Lord...brought you out of the iron-smelting furnace, out of Egypt" (Deut. 4:20). God looked at their time of slavery as an iron-smelting furnace. He saw it as a time of tremendous pressure, of intense heat, of great persecution. When Solomon prayed prayers of dedication for the temple he had built, he spoke of "Your people and Your inheritance, whom You brought out of Egypt, out of that iron-smelting furnace" (1 Kings 8:51). When God confronted His people at a later period in their history through the ministry of Jeremiah, He reminded the prophet that "I brought them out of Egypt, out of the iron-smelting furnace" (Jer. 11:4).

It is difficult for us to imagine the intensity of that kind of a metaphor. It is difficult for us to imagine the cruelty or the unbearable pressure that there must have been on the people. With this iron-smelting furnace, you can almost feel the heat, smell the flame, and get choked on the smoke. It was a time of terrible oppression, and God Himself likened it to a people in a furnace. When the people went into Babylonian captivity, Daniel and his companions were among the first taken away; they were among the choice young men Nebuchadnezzar took away from Jerusalem to Babylon, and during their sojourn there, there came a period where Nebuchadnezzar set up a golden statue. The golden statue, by the way, was sixty cubits high and six cubits wide. Anyone who refused to bow before this wretched idol of evil was to face the horrific death of a fiery furnace. But Daniel's three companions refused to bow down and worship the idol. What they said is a fantastic statement of faith, and it is very relevant to our study of the Book of Revelation. They said:

*If we are thrown into the blazing furnace, the God we serve
is able to save us from it...* (Daniel 3:17).

Now that is a great statement of faith—our God is *able* to
save us,

And he will rescue us from your hand, O king (Daniel 3:17).

Even bolder—not only is our God able but our God *will*.
However, the ultimate statement of faith surely is this one:

*But even if he does not, we want you to know, O king, that
we will not serve your gods or worship the image of gold you
have set up* (Daniel 3:18).

These men had incredible faith. They believed God could,
and they believed God would, but they were prepared for the
fact that God might not, and yet still they would not
compromise, they would not bow. That is the message of the
Book of Revelation. The Book of Revelation is a book for
winners, but here is its great and wondrous enigma. You can
win even if you die! We do not give in under pressure, we do
not give in under persuasion, and we do not give in under
bribery or corruption. We stand firm and, even though they
slay us, yet we win, for "Where, O death, is your victory?
Where, O death, is your sting?" (1 Cor. 15:55). Jesus is alive,
and because He lives we shall live. Jesus' promise and Jesus'
encouragement throughout this book are for a people in a
hostile world, people under persecution, and people being put
to death by the sword and imprisoned in deep dungeons of
great darkness. He is saying, "Be faithful unto death and I will
give you a crown of life." (See Rev. 2:10.) What confidence can
we have in that? Well, because that is what He did—that is the
way He went, the road He trod—and His resurrection is the

guarantee of our eternal life. God does move, in this case, with a deliverance miracle. The men are thrown into the fiery furnace, heated seven times hotter than it ever has been before, such an intense heat that the guards accompanying the prisoners to the door of the furnace die. Nebuchadnezzar takes his ringside seat to watch, and suddenly his eyes pop and his chin drops, and he says, "Look, wasn't it three men we cast into the fire? But I see four men walking unbound and unharmed, and the fourth looks like a son of the gods."

Egypt had been an iron-smelting furnace, Babylon had been a furnace of affliction, but when John sees Jesus and describes Him from His snowy woolly head all the way down to His feet, he notices this: His feet are like bronze that has been caused to glow in a furnace. That is because He had been there. He had been down into the iron-smelting furnace of Egypt, He had stood in the midst of His people, and He had taken the heat Himself and had led them out of their bondage on two great fiery feet. At night you could see the fire, and in the day it looked like a cloud, but the two great legs of Jesus marched out before His people and brought them into deliverance. Nebuchadnezzar saw Him, one like the son of the gods standing in the furnace, and he went and pulled out Shadrach, Meshach, and Abednego. The only thing that had burned was the rope that had bound them, and they came out into the glorious liberty of the sons of God.

The good news about the Book of Revelation is this. He is speaking to His people facing persecution, facing death, to a people under all kinds of intolerable pressures, but He is saying to them, "It is all right, I have taken the heat. I come down into the place where you are. I come down into the furnace of your despair. I come down into the furnace of your heat, and I will bring you out." The good news for us—and this is why we must always approach the Book of Revelation as a devotional book— is that in whatever circumstances we find ourselves, under whatever pressure we are under, whatever furnace we feel we are living, however hot it is getting for us where we are, Jesus says, "I am with you! I am with you to bring you out. I am with you to save you. I am with you to deliver you."

Now, I am sure there are many more acceptable theological reasons why Jesus has feet that look like bronze glowing in a furnace, but I like this one. I like to know that when it is too hot to handle where I am, Jesus is there with the guarantee of bringing me out of my dilemma, out of my pressure, and out of my unbearable difficulty because He is committed to me. That is His message here to this whole church in the first century.

He said to His disciples, "In this world you will have trouble" (John 16:33). Today's church does not like speaking about persecution and pressure and problems and difficulties; it only likes to speak about success and to emphasize progress and peace and prosperity. I believe in all those things, but the Bible is full of persecution and difficulty. And Jesus made this promise: "In this world you will have trouble." I wish He had not said it, but He did. You do not have to be in the Kingdom very long to know it is true. In the world you do have trouble. But then He says, "But take heart! I have overcome the world" (John 16:33).

Revelation is written to overcomers, and I will just make this observation here: you do not need to be an overcomer if there is nothing to overcome! When Jesus challenges us to overcome, it gives me a strong clue that there is some stuff out there that I am going to face that is not going to be a walkover. I need to be prepared for that. I am appalled by the number of believers who seem to go on well, who are the most vocal in the worship, who always give their amen to the message, and then, when trouble comes, collapse in a hopeless heap. They have not been taught that pressure is part of the process. They have not been taught what James taught: "Consider it pure joy, my brothers, whenever you face trials of many kinds, because you know that the testing of your faith develops perseverance. Perseverance must finish its work so that you may be mature and complete, not lacking anything" (James 1:2-4). Paul puts it like this: "We know that in all things God works for the good of those who love Him, who have been called according to His purpose" (Rom. 8:28).

If you do not know that you are called with a purpose, that you have been born into the Kingdom of God with a divine destiny to fulfill, then every problem, every pressure, and every disappointment that comes your way becomes a stumbling block over which you fall. However, if you know that there is a destiny to be fulfilled—if, like your father Abraham, you have seen the city (we will find it at the end of the Book of Revelation and discussed in Volume 2) and know that you have got a destiny there—then the things that were once stumbling blocks that caused you to fall are transformed into stepping stones by which you make progress. Jesus appears in glory in the opening chapter because He wants us to know, "I was dead, but now I am alive forever and ever. I have been where you have been, I have felt what you have felt and I have overcome it all and because I live, you shall live also."

The Speaking Mouth

Let us take another look at this Jesus, not now with His glowing feet but with His speaking mouth. As we read this description of Christ, it is a wonderful, full description, a head-to-foot description, and yet John seems to be drawn magnetically to one particular feature above all the others. The others get a mention, a description, but this one he focuses on three times: the mouth of Jesus. Jesus, although risen and ascended on high, is the Jesus who still speaks. Jesus is the last word from God to the world. The writer of the Hebrews begins his book like this: "In the past God spoke to our forefathers through the prophets at many times and in various ways, but in these last days He has spoken to us by His Son" (Heb. 1:1-2).

Jesus is God's last word; but it is not a word that was heard two thousand years ago and then went silent. It is a word that continues to impact our world. It is a word that is still heard by those who have ears to hear what the Spirit is saying. The writer of the Hebrews not only said God spoke to us through His Son, he also says He upholds all things by His powerful word. You see, the whole of the universe was created with a word, and that word is still speaking; that is why the universe does not fall to pieces. Jesus, who spoke two thousand years ago as the ultimate revelation of God, is still speaking; and John meets Him and is fascinated by His voice. In fact, his first encounter with Christ is a voice behind him, "like a trumpet." He turns to see and, in the midst of the lampstands, he sees the Son of Man and "His voice was like the sound of rushing waters." He looks at Him again and says, "Out of His mouth came a sharp two-edged sword." There are three focuses on the mouth of Christ: the trumpet sound, the mighty rushing waters, and the double-edged sword. All those things communicate to us a Christ who is constantly vocal, a Jesus who speaks.

One of the things the first-century church was learning was how to hear and respond to the voice of God. We, too, need to rediscover first how to hear the voice of God and then how to respond. You and I have probably been in various situations in our lives when we have been in a dilemma, and we have not been sure what to do or which route to take, and we have prayed and nothing has happened. And we have probably said, "I wonder what God is trying to say in this." Well, God never ever tried to say anything. God only ever says things. We treat Him as if He has some kind of speech impediment. If we do not hear, it is not because there is something wrong with God's mouth; the problem lies with our ears. That is what Jesus makes very clear when He writes to the seven churches. He says, "He that has an ear to hear let him hear." We need to learn to hear again the voice of the Spirit, and, having learned how to hear, we need to learn how to speak with the anointing of God. Jesus speaks clearly the word of God, and He speaks it in three different directions.

He speaks with a trumpet voice, and the trumpet voice in Scripture always represents God speaking to His people, God addressing the covenant community, God speaking to the church. Just a cursory reading of Scripture will tell you that. Let me give you just one example. God speaks to Ezekiel. He says, "I have made you a watchman, a prophet-watchman on the wall of the city." What does the watchman do? He blows the trumpet, he warns the people, he prepares the people for what is coming. It is not just an Old Testament picture. Paul, when he is teaching the Corinthians how to move in spiritual gifts and particularly in the gift of prophecy, says to them, "If the trumpet does not sound a clear call, who will get ready for battle?" (1 Cor. 14:8). The trumpet is God speaking to His church. It is how Jesus first addresses John and gets his attention. We need to learn how to blow the trumpet again, how to blow the trumpet in Zion and get the attention of the people of God that they might hear what the Spirit is saying to the church.

Then John said His voice was like the sound of rushing waters. That is a strange concept, a difficult one to handle. However, the same words are used in two other places in the Book of Revelation, in chapter 14 and in chapter 19, and in both places it represents the praise and worship that surrounds the throne of Heaven.

We must understand that there is a prophetic dimension to our praise and worship. When we move prophetically in song and worship and praise, something happens in the Spirit that is inexplicable, but it is dynamic and real. Jesus Himself is pictured as one who speaks with a voice that sounds like rushing waters, which is strange. You think that surely Jesus does not worship in the presence of God, does He? Yes, He does. What is more, the Bible reveals to us that the Father sings. That might be a totally new concept to some of us, but at the end of Zephaniah it says, "The Lord your God is with you, he is mighty to save. He will take great delight in you, he will quiet you with his love, he will rejoice over you with singing" (Zeph. 3:17).

I want to suggest to you that when God sings, God sings prophetically. God sings over you and me not because of what we are now but because of what He knows we will be. He loves us as we are, but He loves us too much to leave us as we are. His ultimate aim is to make us just like His Son, and He has every confidence that He will succeed. Not for a moment does God entertain the thought that He could fail. It has no place in His mind; there is not a possibility, not the slightest or the most extreme chance, that God could fail in anything that He determines to do—and

He is determined to make us like Jesus. He is very happy about this. He actually has more faith in you than you have in yourself. Even if we deny Him, He cannot deny Himself. So He sings over us. What is more, Jesus sings. Hebrews speaks about Him bringing many sons to glory, and He sings prophetically about it for it tells us that "in the presence of the congregation I will sing your praises" (Heb. 2:12). The Son walks in our midst, just as we saw Him standing amongst the lampstands, and He is full of song; He is praising God that what God has begun He will complete. Jesus is full of confidence. We have to learn to sing songs of prophetic worship that declare not only what God has done, not only how we feel, but that declare our confidence in all that God is going to do and to speak back to God the promises He has made.

Then it says that out of His mouth came a sharp two-edged sword, and that sword is God's word to the world. We have to learn to prophesy in these dimensions. We prophesy to each other with the trumpet sound, we prophesy to the Heavens with the sound of rushing waters, and we prophesy to the world with a sharp sword that comes out of our mouths. Later on, in chapter 19, we see Jesus riding out to conquer the world, and out of His mouth comes the sword with which He is going to strike down the nations. Does that mean He is going to kill them? Is this the last battle? Is this Armageddon? No, this is the triumph of the Gospel because He says He will smite them, He will cut them down with the sword of His mouth, and then He will rule over them with an iron scepter. He has no desire to rule over corpses.

Let me give you a clue that will help us understand this. On the day of Pentecost, Peter got up and wielded the sword of the Spirit under great anointing and with such tremendous effect that the people who heard him were cut to their hearts. They died to sin and came alive to God, and what we find in this first portrait of Christ is a Jesus who truly is ruler of the universe. He is a Jesus who has determined to bring His people out of all their afflictions and cause them to be just like Him. He is a Jesus who is determined to bring the world into submission to His lordship. It is a good place to begin. So many people want to rush on and find out who the beast is, but the most important thing is for us to know who Jesus is.

CHAPTER 2

Beginning in Heaven

As I indicated in the last chapter, most people's fascination with the Book of Revelation comes from the more bizarre and horror-comic kind of images often associated with it. Many people, for instance, are solely concerned with identifying the beast. You may well have someone in your church that thinks she is married to him—and that is a far more immediate problem! However, it is much more important for us to know not who the beast is, but who Jesus is. When we know who Jesus is, when we see Him as He really is, then the things that would cause us disturbance and fear are easily dealt with. When we know Him, what can we fear? If God is for us, who can be against us? God is on our side. God is committed to us. God comes down to us in our most desperate situations. He walks in our furnace to deliver us and bring us into freedom. We saw, in John's vision, a Jesus who stood in the midst of the lampstands. Jesus is in the middle of His Church, and it is important that before we get into the blood and the horror—for there is some in the Book of Revelation—that we see Jesus at the center of everything. We must get Jesus in our sights if we are to see anything at all from the right perspective. In this chapter, we are going to look at chapters 4 and 5 of Revelation, because they belong together, making one glorious episode. I would suggest that you read these chapters before you go any further.

John is going to show us some awful things. He is going to reveal to us seven horrendous plagues and uncover terrible things that break out in our earth after seven trumpets have been blown. He will introduce us to antagonists whose one desire is to overcome and destroy the Church of Jesus Christ. He will show us the conflict in which we are engaged and the enemy that we face. But before he ever takes one step in that direction, before he unveils one principle in the whole area of spiritual warfare, before he gives us one glimpse of the enemy, he takes us up into the Heavens.

As Christians, the Heavens are our natural environment. The Bible tells us that you and I were once dead in trespasses and sins. We were enemies of God, separated from Him by sin. We walked under the influence of "the ruler of the kingdom of the air, the spirit who is now at work in those who are disobedient" (Eph. 2:2). But God, who is rich in mercy, whose unfailing love is toward us, whose grace is unfathomable, whose arm was not too short to save, reached down into your horrible pit, the slimy mud of your failure, lifted you out, and didn't just set your feet upon a rock but raised you with Christ and seated you in the Heavenly realms with Jesus! So when John hears a voice that says "Come up here," we too have heard it. We have responded to it. This is not the church being raptured; this is the redeemed being raised to life in Jesus. This is us recognizing that we are seated with Christ in the Heavenly realms, that these realms are our natural environment.

Notice that in Ephesians 2 the devil is referred to as "the ruler of the kingdom of the air." We were earthbound, and so, in a kind of metaphorical sense, we were *under* him. He had the power of the air, and we were earthbound. But now, in Christ, we are no longer earthbound. Nor are we air-bound. We dwell in the Heavens. Once the devil was over us, but now he is under us. Our home, our citizenship, is in Heaven. It is not just a future hope; it is a present reality. We are God's Heavenly people; we are seated in the Heavens in Christ. Now God wants us to realize that we are seated in the Heavens in Christ for a very simple reason: things look much better from up there!

I will have more to say about this Heavenly perspective later on, but it is important first to note once again that Jesus dwells on the center of all things. John has already seen him on the Island of Patmos, in the center of the church, surrounded by the lampstands. Now, in these two chapters, he shows us Jesus as the focal point, the pivot and the crux of the whole universe. Everything has meaning only as it relates to Jesus. Nothing in the universe can function properly until it relates rightly with Christ. You and I were hopeless and helpless until Jesus came into our lives because, although we searched for our identity, for the meaning of life, for the answers to the age-old questions like "Who am I?" and "Why am I here?" none of it is answerable until you meet Jesus. In fact, I have labored so much at the beginning of this book about our need to know Christ for this simple reason—until you know Christ, you cannot even know yourself.

Jesus called His disciples together one day and asked them what the word out on the street about Him was. What were they saying out there? And there were a number of different replies. If there had been a straw poll, there probably would have been as many different answers as there were people. Everybody has got an opinion about Jesus. Everyone is an expert on what Christianity is. There are people who are unbelievers, pagans, some even lacking any sense of morality, but they think they know what Christianity is all about. It never ceases to amaze me how people out in the world can pontificate about what the church should be doing, and yet they have no interest in God and no idea who Jesus is. But one of the problems we face is that there are also people *in the church* who do not really know who Jesus is. They have bowed the knee and come into the Kingdom, acknowledged Him as Lord and been saved, but they do not really know who He is. They still live in fear of demons, they still live under anxiety about the power of the devil, and they are afraid of what is going on in the world. But if you know who Jesus is, those things will never touch you. It is vitally important that we know who Jesus is!

One day, Jesus asked the disciples, "Who do they say I am?" and there were all kinds of responses. He then asked them, "But who do *you* say I am?" Now we are getting down to the thing that really matters. "But what about you?" He asked. "Who do you say I am?" Simon Peter answered, "You are the Christ, the Son of the living God." Jesus replied, "Blessed are you, Simon son of Jonah, for this was not revealed to you by man, but by My Father in heaven. And I tell you that you are Peter, and on this rock I will build My church, and the gates of hades will not overcome it" (Matt. 16:15-18).

This is a fantastic statement. "I am going to build My church and the gates of hell shall not prevail against it," says Jesus. Death may overcome you, but hell never will! But notice how it works: "You are Christ"; "Yes, and you are Peter." Peter doesn't know who he is until he knows who Christ is. He was just Simon, son of Jonah—but now he is Peter. He has a revelation of himself in the light of the revelation he has of Christ. In His light, we see light (Ps. 36:9). We will never know who we are or what God has called us to do until we know who Jesus is. And so unashamedly and without apology, I am spending these opening chapters focusing on Jesus. The Book of Revelation is the book of the revelation of Jesus. And it is a revelation of Jesus that was essential for the first century church. It is also essential for the twenty-first century church so that we can face our world in a way that always leads us in triumph. We need to know who He is so that we can know who we are, and so that we can know what His Church is and what it is here to do.

The Standing Lamb

As you read chapters 4 and 5 in the Book of Revelation, you will notice that there is a kind of repetition all the way through that continually highlights Jesus. We see Him now as the Lamb. There will be more to consider about the Lamb, but let us notice here that it says, "I saw a Lamb, looking as if it had been slain, standing…" (Rev. 5:6). This is an enigma right away. This is a strange, unnatural concept—to see a lamb that had been slain, standing! But this is what God is always communicating to us right through this book—death does not equal defeat, death is

45

not the end. The Lamb has been slain and yet here He is—standing!

Now notice where He is standing. "I saw a Lamb, looking as if it had been slain, standing in the center of the throne" (Rev. 5:6). This is also a strange expression. We would have understood it if it said He was just *sitting* on the throne. It would have spoken volumes about His lordship, His power and authority, His triumph, and His relationship with the Father. If it had said He was sitting *on the edge* of the throne, that could have communicated something of the anticipation of His return.

But it does not say that. It tells us that He is *standing in the center* of the throne; that is because even the throne revolves around Jesus. He is in the center of all God's purpose. Too many authors have marginalized Jesus in this book and emphasized things that should never have been emphasized. God's will, as I have stated already, is that, in all things, Jesus should have the preeminence; and here He is even in the center of the throne of God. I do not know what the throne looks like. We get something of a description, but it is all imagery and symbol. We cannot really know what the throne is like, but we know this—Jesus occupies the center place in the throne of God.

Four Living Creatures

Not only is Jesus in the center of the throne, but the same verse tells us that He is encircled by the four living creatures. These four strange creatures occur occasionally in the Word of God; they are the cherubim that Ezekiel sees actually carrying the throne of Jesus as they pursue his purpose in the world. They are primarily guardians of the throne, and they surround the throne. There are four of them, and four is an important number. We will look at some numbers as we go through the Book of Revelation together, but four is one of the most important numbers because four speaks of the world. That is why from the Garden of Eden a river arose, and as it flowed out, it broke into four rivers because God's purpose was for the blessing of the garden to flow to the four corners of the earth. That has always been God's will. God wants our whole world turned into a garden. In fact, at the end we find it is a city *and* a garden—a strange combination. God is concerned with our earth, and it is interesting that those closest to His throne are those who dynamically represent His world, because God is not the author of the distance between the world and His throne. It is sin that has opened the gulf, and, as Abraham says to Lazarus, there is "a great chasm" between them (Luke 16:26). There is a chasm, a gulf; but the Book of Revelation, and indeed the whole New Testament, is about how God bridges the gulf between His throne and His world.

Now, these four living creatures are interesting. One looks like a man; we can cope with that. One looks like a calf or a bull; that's a bit of a challenge. One looks like an eagle and one like a lion. In fact, in Ezekiel each of them has four faces. They have a face at the front, a face at the back and a face on both sides. That is why they can go straight ahead whichever way they go. When you have four faces, *everywhere you go* is forward. When you have four faces, you *always* see eye to eye; you cannot help it. But here they are shown in a different guise, and each one of them has one of those faces. The old rabbis used to teach something about this, and I think there is great truth in it. They taught that the bull is the lord of all domesticated animals, the lion is the lord of all wild beasts, the eagle is the lord of all the birds of the air, and man is the lord of all the creation of God. Yet all of them stand subservient to His throne. There is a picture here of a world restored, a world back in harmony, delivered from its corruption, taken out of its spoil and its decay, and coming through to a real, divine ecology. Everything is in harmony again under the throne of God, and the only way our world, our physical world, will be redeemed is as men acknowledge the lordship of Jesus Christ. So we see a restored creation cooperating in bringing the throne of God into every circumstance and situation. But these creatures are represented to us as encircling the throne, for they too have their focus on Jesus. They too look to Him. They too take their command from Him. They do His bidding.

The Rainbow

So Jesus is at the center of the throne, and four living creatures surround the throne. But we see, in chapter 4, that around the throne was a rainbow. The rainbow throughout Scripture is a picture of God's covenant. In fact, it does not appear until the ninth chapter of Genesis, when God hangs it in the sky as a sign of His covenant—not only with Noah and his descendants, but with all of creation. God has made a covenant with inanimate earth. God has made a covenant with the creatures that walk or crawl or fly in our universe. God has made a covenant with the whole of His creation. The sign of that covenant is the rainbow. God said to Noah, "Whenever the rainbow appears in the clouds, I will see it and remember the everlasting covenant between God and all living creatures of every kind on the earth" (Gen. 9:16).

The problem with that, of course, is that we do not always see the rainbow. There have to be the right kind of meteorological conditions in order for us to see the rainbow. You have to have the sun shining and at least heavy moisture in the air, if not rain. You have to have the right conditions to see the rainbow. We occasionally see it, but not frequently, and therefore you could sit and wonder if God forgets his covenant. And yet when we get a glimpse into the Heavens, we discover that God sees the rainbow all the time because it surrounds his throne. It is not actually a rainbow, in the sense of a bow. It is a full circle. It actually totally surrounds the throne upon which He sits, because every covenant God has ever made revolves around Jesus. All the covenants were covenants of promise. Paul tells us that when we were sinners, when we were separate from God and Christ, we were strangers to the covenants of promise (Eph. 2:12). That tells us that all the covenants God made were covenants of promise. And the picture of the rainbow surrounding Jesus on the throne tells me this: they all become relevant when I come into a relationship with Jesus, because they all speak of Him.

We will look at the covenants later when we come to Chapter 10 and see one of the wonderful pictures of Christ. We will need to talk about the covenants that God has made through history and the covenant into which He has brought us. But for now, let us note that the rainbow encircles the throne. God remembers His covenant. In fact, God looks at everything through the colors of His covenant. God looks at you through the covenant. You may think you are bland, you may think you are ordinary, you may think you are nothing special, but every time God looks at you, He sees you through the multicolored grace of His covenant. He sees you in technicolor! He sees you in brilliant light. He sees you and remembers His covenant.

Twenty-four Elders

Also surrounding the throne were twenty-four other thrones, and on them sat twenty-four elders. We are looking here at the government of God's people. One of the other numbers that we

49

will have to look at because it carries such great significance is the number twelve. It is a very important number in the Book of Revelation because it speaks of God's Kingdom or God's government, and "twelve" conveys that throughout Scripture. That is why we have twelve patriarchs in the Old Testament, and twelve judges are recorded in the book of that name. It is why we have twelve apostles in the New Testament. In our Bible we have twelve minor prophets. It does not mean they were insignificant, only that they wrote smaller books than the others. So we have these twelve minor prophets, which the rabbis used to call "the Twelve." This gives us an idea why Jesus called his disciples "the Twelve": they, too, were going to carry His prophetic word to the world. But He used "twelve" to use the number of God's government and His Kingdom. Twelve times two is twenty-four. We see these twenty-four thrones in Heaven, and it teaches us that God governs His Kingdom through delegated authority. Do you remember that Psalm that says, "I rejoiced with those who said to me, 'Let us go to the house of the Lord.' Our feet are standing in your gates, O Jerusalem. Jerusalem is built like a city that is closely compacted together" (Ps. 122:1-3). "There," continues the Psalmist, "the thrones [note the plural] for judgment stand, the thrones of the house of David" (Ps. 122:5). There is one throne, but from that throne comes delegated authority, and so the Psalmist refers to thrones in the plural.

Now, delegated authority only works when it is focused on Jesus; true delegated authority will never lord it over the flock. It will not seek to build its own empire. It will always turn people to Jesus. I like the way these elders are described in the Book of Revelation, and they appear in several sections of the book. They are seated on thrones, so they do have authority. They are wearing golden crowns, so they do have power. There is no question about that. But every time they think of Jesus, every time the four creatures give them an excuse or an opportunity, they get off their thrones, fall on their faces, take off their crowns, and throw them at the feet of the Lamb. True leaders always know how to worship Jesus because they are focused on Him; they surround His throne. And every one of these elders looks at the Lamb. They have their vision filled with the Lamb. They are sensitive to the moving of the Spirit in the presence of the Lamb. They have given themselves away to the Lamb. They do not think that they have a right to sit on their thrones. They do not believe that the crowns are riveted to their foreheads. They are ready to cast them down and fall on their faces and give worship to Him who lives forever and ever because everything revolves around the Lamb. They have not done a bit of surreptitious furniture removal and put His throne in the corner. It is always in the center, and they surround His throne and look to Him. It is not about you. It is not about me. It is all about Jesus.

Multitudes of Angels

The chapter continues: "Then I looked and heard the voice of many angels, numbering thousands upon thousands, and ten thousand times ten thousand. They encircled the throne and the living creatures and the elders" (Rev. 5:11). Every angelic being, every archangel and angel, all the cherubim and seraphim, all the hosts of Heaven surround the throne of Jesus. The writer of the Hebrews takes great pains to remind us that Jesus is far greater than the angels, that He is exalted far above the angels. He has a name that no angel can hope to approach. And all the angels of Heaven, all the servants of God, all those ministering spirits surround and crowd in around the throne; they see the Lamb and they worship Him.

If we were to take a stone and drop it in a pool, you know what would happen. You have watched it, I am sure: the ripples move out and out and out. And so it is with Jesus upon His throne. It is as if a holy stone had been set in the midst of the pool of our universe, and the ripple effect has gone out and out and out and out; but it all surrounds and emanates from the throne, and from Him who sits upon the throne, who lives forever and ever. Everything, everything, but everything, revolves around Jesus.

Heaven and Earth

As we move on in this prophetic book, we are going to see a world in rebellion. We catch up with some of the events that are going on in our universe, with sin and wickedness. We see deception and cruelty, and persecution and death. But it is here that we see the real picture. It is here that we face the ultimate reality. It is here that we need to begin our pilgrimage. You see this is not our destiny; this is where we begin. We do not struggle through our troubles hoping that somewhere along the way we will get a glimpse of what God is really after. We begin with a revelation of who He is, and we move with confidence from that moment. You can tackle anything if you have been to this place. You can handle any situation if you have spent time here, with John, in the presence of the Lord who is in the center of His throne, surrounded by four living creatures, encircled by a rainbow, surrounded by twenty-four elders on thrones, and by multitudes of angels. I can handle any situation because it does not end there, either. "Then I heard every creature in heaven and on earth and under the earth and on the sea, and all that is in them, singing" (Rev. 5:13). We are going to hear them cry. We are going to hear them yelling. We are going to hear them cursing. We are going to hear them blaspheming. But this is the actual reality. The earth is reserved to worship God. The earth is designed to bring glory to its creator. Here is the reality. The whole of creation is singing, "To Him who sits on the throne and to the Lamb be praise and honor and glory and power, for ever and ever!" (Rev. 5:13). Then "The four living creatures said, 'Amen,' and the elders fell down and worshiped" (Rev. 5:14). That is the reality of the world in which we live. It isn't fantasy or make believe. It isn't myth, legend, or wishful thinking. This is reality. It is not to deny the troubles in our world, the pain and the disappointment, the hunger and the tragedy. It is not to deny that these exist, but it is to say this: it is destined to change. For in the purpose of God, "The kingdom of the world has become the kingdom of our Lord and of his Christ, and He will reign for ever and ever" (Rev. 11:15). Our world is not reserved for disaster but for deliverance. It is not reserved to wither and die, but to be made new in the power of the Lord Jesus Christ. John begins right here, before a beast has roared, before a false prophet has spoken, before a plague has come, before a trumpet has sounded. He says this is where we begin—in the Heavenlies. This is where it all comes from. Satan is not in charge of the world. Satan has not written the agenda. Satan does not have a plan that he is pursuing to its ultimate goal and that will succeed. Our God is a God who reigns, who has all things in His power, and He has a determined purpose that will be fulfilled. And whatever satan seeks to do, he only does it ultimately to further the purposes of God.

Perceiving God's Purpose

When Jesus died, He was crucified by the Romans. Peter tells us that He was delivered to godless hands. It was the Roman Empire, and the power of Caesar and all the battalions of Rome, that were responsible for nailing Him to the cross. But behind the Romans were the Jews who pressured and persuaded them to crucify Him. Behind the Jews was Judas who betrayed Him. Behind Judas was satan who entered Him. But behind satan was God! For Peter stands up on the day of Pentecost and says, "This man was handed over to you by God's set purpose and foreknowledge; and you, with the help of wicked men, put Him to death by nailing Him to the cross" (Acts 2:23). Revelation reveals Jesus as the Lamb slain before the foundation of the world. God had a plan. God had a purpose. It was formulated in the courts of Heaven before the world was made. It was brought together in the council rooms of eternity before man ever stood on the world or sin came to corrupt the creation of God. There was a plan laid. There was a Son ready. There was a will formulated and put into action at the right time; and everything that has happened, everything that is happening, and everything that will yet happen is all part of the great mystery of the plan of God that will ultimately redound to His glory as every creature under Heaven joins in the great chorus, the universal celebration, the acclamation of Him who sits upon the throne.

He is the Lord, the creator and the sustainer of all things. When John takes us up into Heaven, he is not representing a church raptured out of the world so that the devil can take over and run amok in the creation of God. He is showing us what happened to each one of us when we repented and believed the Gospel, when we came to faith in Jesus and were seated with Him in the Heavenly realms. From there we look down from the vantage point of eternity, and say, "Ha! I thought that was a problem, but it was part of the purpose; I thought that was a setback, but it was a strategy for divine advance; I thought that was persecution, but it was just the way God brought purity to his people; I thought that was a disaster, but it was God moving, manipulating, and juggling the affairs of our world to bring everything into a glorious pattern of divine purpose and ultimate fulfillment." You and I have been caught up in the drama of the ages. You and I are part of a purpose that had its beginnings in the unfathomable depths of God's mind, in the eternities that are behind us. We may not see it come to its fullness in our lifetime, but we nevertheless have a part to play in order to see it fulfilled. If we will see God's purpose and throw ourselves unreservedly into being part of it, we can see it move forward in our generation.

CHAPTER 3

Jesus and John

The Book of Revelation helps us understand how God fulfills His purpose. We begin with Jesus encountering John. He meets an individual. He meets His servant. From there He goes on to address the churches in chapters 2 and 3, the seven churches of Asia. From there He goes on to impact the world. In a sense, that is how God has always furthered His purpose. He begins with the individual. From the individual He affects the Church, and the Church then goes on the affect the world. What God shows us in this plan of the book is how He still operates in our own generation. God wants to meet with you, and God wants to meet with me, individually. We have a very intimate and personal relationship with God, and God will not violate that. God wants to maintain and enlarge that relationship we have with Him and cause it to grow. When you and I are right with God, and each individual in the Church is right with God, then the Church itself as an entity is right with God. When the Church is right with God, the world will be changed by the influence of the Church.

There is a very powerful historical parable of this principle in the Scriptures, and it happened on the day of Pentecost. You will remember that it tells us that "they were all together in one place" and then "a sound like the blowing of a violent wind came from heaven" and every one of them, each individual, was filled with the Spirit, and they all began to speak with other tongues as the Spirit enabled them (Acts 2:1-4). There was an encounter—a personal and intimate encounter with the Holy Spirit—for each individual who was there in that upper room. Not only did the Holy Spirit impact each individual, but also the whole Church was filled with the Spirit. The violent rushing wind that came from Heaven filled the whole *house*. God's purpose for us as individuals is that we be filled with the Holy Spirit. But more than that, His purpose is to fill the whole house.

As you look down through history at God's dealings with His people, for example, when He first had them erect a tabernacle and then later a temple, His approval was always demonstrated by a manifestation of His presence. A cloud filled the house, and God's presence was so dynamic that even their prearranged programs had to be abandoned. They were overwhelmed by the sense of the presence of God. The priests could not minister. Nothing could happen because God had demonstrated His presence in the midst of his people. I long for days like that. I long for days when we abandon our program, when the preacher does not preach his sermon, when the musician does not pick up his instrument, not because I despise or reject those things, but because more important than any of those things is the presence of God—the presence of God that overawes us, that silences us, that causes us to fall down and worship Him. That is what I long for. That is what I desire. Some of you reading this have had fleeting moments of that. Some of you have had past encounters that are both awesome and memorable—and having been there, you know that nothing else will ever satisfy you.

However, when God fills the Church, he does it so that he might impact the world. Luke carefully records for us in Acts that, at that time, there were devout men dwelling in Jerusalem "from every nation under heaven" (Acts 2:5). So the enacted parable is this: every person filled, the whole house filled, the whole world impacted. And it is this same pattern that we see in the Book of Revelation. Jesus meets with John, he comes to the Church, and, from the Church, he moves out to touch the world.

John, the Trouble-Maker

It is my conviction that this book was written before A.D. 70, and by the apostle John. The writer is John the disciple, the apostle, and he is probably, by this time, the last surviving apostle of the Lamb. It is most likely that every other one of the twelve has laid down his life in martyrdom for Jesus. Even Paul has probably gone home to his reward, and by this time only John is left, an old man, well into his mature years. But what I like about him is that he is still giving the world a lot of trouble! He is on Patmos because of the Word of God. These islands strung out in the Aegean Sea, of which Patmos was one, were used as penal colonies for those who had offended the policies of the Roman Empire. Those who had dared to stand against the will of Rome often found themselves exiled to these rocky islands. That is probably why John is there. John the old man has been upsetting the status quo, causing problems for the powers that be, having so much impact on the power of the Roman Empire that he has been put out of the way and removed from his sphere of influence.

From this there are two very important things to take on board. Firstly, you are never disqualified from the service of Christ through age. There is no retirement program in Heaven. John has not thought for a moment that the time has come to hang up his Bible. He is there because of the Word of God. He is a man consumed by the Word, obsessed by the Word, zealous for the Word; he is determined to preach Christ, and the preaching of Christ has got him into trouble—and the true preaching of Christ will always get you into trouble. Secondly, he has offended society, offended those who do not want things changed, challenged, or affected. But we are a people who are called by God to challenge the status quo, to challenge society. We are called to challenge the moral state of the nation in which we live. We are not just to challenge it in a negative sense, but to offer a viable alternative that says that there is a Kingdom in which you can live in peace and joy in the Holy Spirit and know the righteousness of God that brings the happiness of Heaven into our world. John is doing that, and because of that he has been exiled.

John, Brother and Fellow-servant

I like the way John introduces himself. I guess he is writing it after he has seen all his visions, and, although he is John the apostle, the man of great influence and respect in the churches, he introduces himself as John, "your brother" (Rev. 1:9). I believe in the recognition of ministry, in apostles and prophets, evangelists, pastors and teachers. I believe in receiving a prophet in the name of a prophet because that is how we get the prophet's reward. I believe in receiving men with honor, but I do not believe in putting men on a pedestal. I don't believe in men who are out of reach, who live on some other planet and in some other atmosphere. I believe in men and women who are first and foremost brothers and sisters in the things of God. John is just a brother. Sometimes out of great respect and genuine love we get introduced in extravagant ways. I do it myself sometimes. I remember introducing a visiting preacher at our congregation in rather glowing terms. He got up and said there were two people in the meeting who immediately needed to repent: "Tony, for introducing me like he did, and me, for enjoying it." The bottom line is that we are just brothers—brothers and companions. That is, we are not just those who are related, but those who share in a common task, those who are yoked together for a common purpose. John sees every saint, every servant of Christ, whether he has a title or no title, whether he has a recognized ministry or not, as those who are companions in the work of God. Paul would call them yokefellows.

We are all necessary. We are all vital. It is not just about the apostles and the prophets; it is about the servants of Christ, and that is one area in which we all qualify. When I read my Bible, I do not find anywhere that when I stand before the judgment seat of Christ to receive commendation, I will hear, "Well done, good and faithful apostle." I do not find a verse anywhere that says, "Well done, good and faithful prophet." I do not find any chapter that contains the words, "Well done, good and faithful evangelist," "Well done, good and faithful pastor," "Well done, good and faithful teacher," "Well done, good and faithful elder." I cannot find such phrases anywhere; but I can find this: "Well done good and faithful *servant.*" We are on a level playing field when we stand before Christ. We will not be judged on how far we traveled in ministry, nor on how many sermons we preached, how many invitations we responded to, how many conferences we notched up on our Bible. We will be judged on how we served the Lord.

We are companions in the things of God. There is no one person more important than any other, and even as servants, when we have done all that we can do, "We are unworthy servants; we have only done our duty" (Luke 17:10). When you compare what we are and what we can do with the price He paid for us, no one will ever be profitable, and yet we are here by the grace of God.

Companion in Suffering

"I [am] your brother and companion in the suffering" (Rev. 1:9). John introduces suffering right at the beginning of the book. He wants us to know that suffering is not an odd thing that happens. He wants us to know that suffering is not what comes to those who are outside the will of God. You can hear preachers preach like that: "If you are under pressure, if you are in problems, if you are suffering, you are outside the will of God." My Bible nowhere has that kind of teaching. My Bible tells me, and it is the underlying theme of Revelation, "There is trouble out there!" There is suffering to go through. There are sufferings that "are ours in Jesus." This is how John puts it: Suffering is yours. It does not belong to somebody else and is put on you. It is yours. It is yours for this reason. It will do you good. It will cause you to be strong. It is part of the process of God whereby we become more like Jesus. We live in an age where the Church needs to get back to that Scripture where we are told, "You have forgotten that word of encouragement that addresses you as sons." We live in a church that has forgotten the exhortation that speaks to us: "My son, do not make light of the Lord's discipline, and do not lose heart when he rebukes you." Why? The response comes, "because the Lord disciplines those he loves, and he punishes everyone he accepts as a son" (Heb. 12:5-6). If you don't have that discipline, then you are bastards and not sons.

We live in a church that despises discipline, that rejects hardship, that will have nothing to do with suffering, because we believe that the blessing of God is upon us. We believe that the prosperity of God will overwhelm us. We believe that the joy of the Lord will be our strength. Now, all those things are true, but it is not either/or with God. Peter quoted on the day of Pentecost, "In the last days, God says, I will pour out my Spirit on all people" (Acts 2:19). In the last days there is going to be an unprecedented outpouring of the Holy Spirit. But Paul writes to Timothy and says, "There will be terrible times in the last days" (2 Tim. 3:1). Now we might think, "Make up your mind; is it Holy Spirit or terrible times?" The answer is both! It is knowing both how to be in need and how to have plenty (Phil. 4:12) that brings us to the fullness of the blessings of God. Paul wrote this to the Philippians, "For it has been granted to you [as if it were a gift or a prize!] on behalf of Christ not only to believe on him, but also to suffer for him" (Phil. 1:29). To the Thessalonians he writes, "You suffered from your own countrymen the same things those churches suffered from the Jews" (1 Thess. 2:14). Or to the Corinthians, "If we are comforted, it is for your comfort, which produces in you patient endurance of the same sufferings we suffer. And our hope for you is firm, because we know that just as you share in our sufferings, so also you share in our comfort" (2 Cor. 1:6). God is the God who comforts us in all our troubles, but if you do not have troubles, how will you know his comfort? How will you know the patient endurance that is ours in Christ? We need a reality check, a wake-up call, to signal that it is not a sign of being unspiritual to suffer hardship. It is not a sign that you are backsliding because you are going through difficulty. It is a sign that God is disciplining you. It is a sign that you have been accepted as a son and are being shaped into His likeness.

We need to recapture these ancient truths that the Church has jettisoned in its desire for instant everything. We are on a pilgrimage, and sometimes it is through the wilderness, sometimes it is through the valley of the shadow of death, and sometimes it is through the dark and hard place, but always it is *through.* Never is it to dwell there forever. There are some things in our lives that we are not supposed to enjoy. There are some things we just endure; but, like Jesus, we endure for the joy that is set before us. Sorrow lasts for the night, but joy comes in the morning (Ps. 30:5). Do not despise the disciplines of God. Do not be surprised when pain comes. It is from a faithful hand. The apostle Peter also speaks of suffering. He says that we should not suffer as evildoers, and we all acknowledge that. But he goes on to say that if someone suffers in the will of God, they should commit their soul to Him as to a faithful creator (1 Pet. 5:19). Do you know why? It is because, in the suffering, the Creator does His creative work.

I remember when I was at Bible School, in 1965. I was in school when Pastor Richard Wurmbrand was released from a Communist prison in Romania, and he came to visit our college. It was one of the first places he visited after his release. He spoke to us about his suffering, of his solitary confinement, of the revelations he had of God in a lonely, dark, and dank prison cell. As he spoke, he said these words that have lived with me ever since: "A diamond is just a piece of coal that has been under intense pressure and a pearl is only the tear of an oyster." Here was a man who had been through suffering, who had experienced pain, but who had come out refined like gold from the crucible.

We embrace suffering. We do not develop a martyr complex, but we do not run from it. We do not bury our head in the sand; we do not try to carry this unreal "positive confession" in the midst of heartbreaking tragedy. We confess the goodness of God, but we do not try to make our suffering some kind of happy moment. Tears are legitimate, groans are real, and sighs communicate with God.

"Your companion in suffering in patient endurance that are ours in Christ Jesus." (See Rev. 1:9.) So everything that happens to you is yours. It is not somebody else's that fell on you. It is not satan that hurt you. It is not a demon that afflicted you. Everything that happens to you is yours; you possess it because, in your possessing and owning it, it does what God wants it to do. Here is how Paul described it to the Corinthians. He is speaking about receiving different ministries, but in his revelation he moves off into whole new areas that are sometimes difficult for us to understand. He says, "All things are yours, whether Paul or Apollos or Cephas or the world or life or death or the present or the future—all are yours, and you are of Christ, and Christ is of God" (1 Cor. 3:21). All things are yours, life with its pressures as well as its blessings; it is all yours. It is all given to you for a purpose, and therefore we embrace it with faith. All things are yours.

In the Spirit

John knows who he is and he knows why he is on Patmos, and here is the great thing: He may be exiled. He may be separated from his family, his fellowship, and his friends. He may be in solitary confinement, or a chain gang. I don't know exactly what is happening to him, but I know he is restricted in some way. Every door seems to be closed, and every window seems to be barred. There seems to be no way out and no way forward. He is suffering, and he is in discomfort. He is an old man in a penal colony. This is not a good place to be, not a thing to enjoy. He is incarcerated, enclosed, imprisoned. But no matter how they imprison him in the natural, Heaven is open to him. He says that he was on Patmos, but he was "in the Spirit" (Rev. 1:10)! Your circumstance, your situation, or your condition is no obstacle to you being in the Spirit. Your circumstance is no disqualification to God opening the Heavens to you. You can be shut in, but as far as God is concerned, you are wide open. There is no restriction, no prison door that will hold Him. It seems to me that the only problem He has is with us.

I love the story of Peter when he is in prison. The church prays for him, but the church praying for him does not seem to be filled with faith. He is at the door and they are still praying and the little girl comes to tell them that he is at the door and they tell her she is crazy; he must be in prison because they are praying for him (Acts 12:12-17). I am sure they are praying extravagant prayers about walls falling down, iron bars yielding, and gates flying open, and yet they still don't believe it. But God answered their prayers anyway! It tells us this: the angel turned up in prison, the chains fell off, the angel led him out, and the gate opened all by itself. It always amazes me that he could get out of the prison but couldn't get into the prayer meeting! Sometimes the biggest problem that God has is not with the world, but with the Church. The world has no option. God says open, and open it goes. God asks us to open—and we reply, "We'll think about it." But whatever restriction you are in, it is no restriction to God.

"I was in the Spirit," says John. Being in the Spirit is a kind of technical term in the Scriptures that means moving into a new dimension, seeing things that are invisible when in the natural. However, the New Testament also makes it very clear that being in the Spirit should be our natural environment. When Jesus speaks to the woman at the well, He says that those who worship God should worship in the Spirit and in truth (John 4:23). In the Spirit is where we belong. When you worship God, I trust that you don't just sing songs; we are meant to move into a new dimension. Pray, says Jude, pray in the Spirit (Jude 20). I trust that you do not say prayers, but that you pray in the Spirit, because in the Spirit is where we are meant to be. And being in the Spirit when we come together would transform what happens in our gatherings. It means, of course, preparing yourself. You cannot be in the Spirit if you come in a hurry. You cannot be in the Spirit if you come in the midst of an argument. You cannot be in the Spirit if you are full of bad temper when you arrive at the meeting. You cannot be in the Spirit if you have just beaten the kids up in the parking lot. It is difficult at times to be in the Spirit, but when we come together as the people of God, we need to be prepared.

I will tell you what transformed it for me: It was when I understood that the meeting is not the place in which *I* invite Jesus to come, or *I* invite the Holy Spirit to come. The meeting is where *God* invites the Church into *His* presence. John said that he heard the voice that said, "Come up here." Do you know that every time we join together as God's people, we hear a voice that says "Come up here"? We ascend the hill of the Lord. They used to do it literally in the Old Testament. They would actually go up the hill of the Lord; they ascended into His presence, and they climbed a mountain. They knew what they were doing. It was a physical reality for them. They were so fit, too, that they sang on the way up! They had songs for climbing a mountain to. They were called, in

the Scriptures, the "Songs of Ascent." They went into the presence
of God, and they knew what they were doing. They asked, "Who is
going to go up?" "I rejoiced with those who said to me, 'Let us go
to the house of the Lord'" (Ps. 122:1). And they also asked, "Who
can go up?" And they answered, "He who has clean hands and a
pure heart" (Ps. 24:4). They had to get ready. They did not just
amble into the presence of God. They came with a sense of awe
and expectation. They did not gather around the foot of the
mountain for a coffee and then think, "We are ten minutes late;
perhaps we'd better get up there now." No. They came to meet
with God. And that is what happens to us. Hebrews tells us we
have come to Mount Zion (Heb. 12:22). Every time we meet
together we go up a hill. Even if you meet in a cellar, you go up a
hill. You are ascending the hill of the Lord and coming into the
presence of God. And you come in the Spirit. John is in the Spirit
on the Lord's Day.

Certain things happen when you are in the Spirit. In fact, we
will find three other times in this Book of Revelation when John
is in the Spirit. He is in the Spirit when he goes up into the
Heavens. He says immediately that he was in the Spirit and he
saw the throne (Rev. 4:2). Later on, one of the angels says to him,
"Come, I will show you the punishment of the great prostitute,"
and he says, "Then the angel carried me away in the Spirit" (Rev.
17:1-3). Toward the end of the book, another angel says, "Come,
I will show you the bride, the wife of the Lamb," and again he
says, "He carried me away in the Spirit" (Rev. 21:9-10). In the
Spirit, he sees Jesus down here on Earth in the midst of His
Church. In the Spirit, he sees the Lamb upon the throne surrounded by all the hosts of Heaven and the universe. In the
Spirit, he sees the deceptive, seductive prostitute unmasked for
what she really is. And in the Spirit, he sees the bride in all her

purity and in all her glory. We have to be in the Spirit to see those things, to understand what is right and what is wrong, to see what is real and what is counterfeit, to know what is glorious and what is just glittering. We need to be in the Spirit to realize those things. They are discerned in the Spirit.

But other things happen. John says, "I was in the Spirit, and I heard…" (Rev. 1:10). It is when you are in the Spirit that you hear, because it is the Spirit who is speaking. Notice again and again in the letters to the churches in chapters 2 and 3, it ends with, "He who has an ear, let him hear what the Spirit says to the churches." The Spirit is speaking, and the best way to hear the Spirit is to be in the Spirit.

There is a great story in the Old Testament that I love very much; it is in the Book of Judges and is about a man called Gideon. Gideon is a great hero. God calls him to ministry, but his ministry is not on some far and distant isle. It is not to remote and unknown continents or foreign and fearful empires that God calls him. The first thing God has him do is pull down the altar in his own backyard. That's a challenge. It is always easier to be a hero away from home. Every preacher is a great preacher when they are in another country. It is tough on your own turf. Jesus said, "Only in his hometown and in his own house is a prophet without honor" (Matt. 13:57). It is hard to be real and spiritual where you live, where everyone knows you—especially when they have known you since you were a kid! That is a terrible burden to live with. But that is where we have to prove ourselves, where people know us, not where we can go and put on a face, act, or mask. Gideon has to face the issue in his own backyard. He does it at night because he is scared, but he does it anyway.

He pulled down the altar of baal and cut down the Asherah Pole, and then the story continues—the very next thing to happen, a knee-jerk reaction from satan, is that the enemy invades the land. The Edomites, the Amalakites, and all the children of the East in this great confederation of evil invade the land of Canaan, which is the gift of God to His people. The enemy has come into the land. It seems like an overreaction. It seems like overkill. All he did was pull down the altar, and it brings an invasion. Satan will always overreact to whatever we do. He does it not to show his strength but to display his fear. Do you know satan is scared of Jesus? And because satan is scared of Jesus, satan is scared of a church that will take its stand on the Word of God. So we have this overreaction.

And then the story continues. What is God's answer? What is God's strategy? What plan will God hatch now to counteract the invading army? It says that God's Spirit came on Gideon. God's strategy is always an anointing. We will look at that in more depth. We will have a whole chapter about the Church and the Holy Spirit in the Book of Revelation because, although He does not get a huge amount of mention, you will find Him active everywhere throughout the book. He is God's agent on the earth. He is executing the purposes of God in every nation under Heaven.

So the Spirit of the Lord comes on Gideon. This is a strange episode, a kind of a comical verse. It says, "Then the Spirit of the Lord came upon Gideon, and he blew a trumpet" (Judg. 6:34). You would think that you would want to do a bit more than that, but he blew a trumpet. Remember, the trumpet is God's word to His people, and He is sending out a call for the army of God. Notice what happens. The Spirit of the Lord comes upon him and he blows a trumpet. There is no better time to speak the Word of God than when the Spirit of God is upon you. I guess you are like me; I go to conferences and to meetings, and I have a little prayer in my heart and my prayer is this: "O God please let the preacher be under the anointing." I have been in too many meetings when he is not. Or perhaps I will add a little rider: "Let him be under the anointing, but, if he isn't, then at least let him be funny." If you have any sense, then you will pray this prayer, too. Why? Because when the preacher is under the anointing, the Word comes in a different dimension. It doesn't just inform your head, it inspires your heart. It doesn't just give you knowledge, it stirs your spirit. Something is going on inside, and sometimes you cannot even explain what it is, but the Word is coming like flaming arrows into your soul. It may not be eloquent, it may not be well put together, it may not come with the right vocabulary, but it is working in the Holy Ghost. It is nothing other than deep calling to deep. That is what happens when the preacher is under the anointing.

But the preacher, if he is any kind of preacher, also has a prayer that he prays when he comes to speak to the people. And it is this: "O God, let these people be in the Spirit." Why? Because that is when you hear. There are different kinds of hearing. There is a hearing with our physical ears, but there is a hearing that goes on deep down in your spirit. There is a seeing with physical eyes, but there is a seeing with the eyes of the heart. It is what revelation is made of. It is hearing things that do not just go in your ears, but that settle in your heart. It is seeing things that do not just fill your eyes, but inspire you on the inside. It is seeing and hearing in the Spirit.

Still Being Changed

So the Spirit comes on Gideon and he blows the trumpet, and John is in the Spirit and he hears the trumpet. The best place to hear is in the Spirit. That is where you will not only hear but you will understand. I was in the Spirit and I heard. The strange thing is, if I am right about the authorship of this book, if it is John the apostle, the disciple who was part of that intimate trio that went with Jesus into situations from which others were excluded; if it is John who described himself, in his Gospel, as the disciple whom Jesus loved, who leaned on the breast of Jesus at the last Supper; if it is this same John who wrote such a profound and insightful Gospel, who wrote inspiring and encouraging epistles; if it is this same John now exiled on the isle of Patmos because of the Word of God and the testimony of Jesus, you would think at least that when the Lord turned up he would be looking the right way! But he says, "I heard behind me" (Rev. 1:10).

It is almost the stuff of pantomime—"He's behind you!"—but it tells me this: every time we encounter Christ, we must be turned, to be changed. It tells me this: just because you have been around for a long time, just because you have been faithful in ministry, just because you have been successful in what God has called you to do, it is no guarantee that you are still looking in the right direction. Jesus comes to adjust us all the time, to adjust us to His Word. I hope that as you read this book and feel God speaking to you, you are adjusted, you are turned around, because unless we are looking the right way, we will not go in the right direction. John himself hears a voice behind him, and he turns himself and lines himself up with the word he has heard. You may read things in this book that are controversial, that are diametrically opposed to things that you have always believed, and that will challenge you. I am not saying that you must receive every word that comes. You search the Scriptures like the Bereans and check that these things are true (Acts 17:11). But you will hear things from the Spirit because He wants you to turn around. He wants you to change and look in another direction because He has new things yet to lead you into.

CHAPTER 4

Called to Conquer

In the last chapter, we left John in mid-turn. John had turned around to see the voice that had spoken to him. Every time we come together, God wants to turn us to be in line with His Word so that our lives are reflecting what He is saying. John says he turned to see the voice and, having turned, he saw seven golden lampstands. He turned to see Jesus, but he saw the Church because one of the things that this book will teach us is that, although Jesus is still speaking, His communication now comes through the Church. Later on we are going to see John turn to see a Lion, but he sees a Lamb, and just as the Lamb is the Lion, so Christ is the Church. We are the Christ of God in the world, and it is through us that God now speaks. John sees, in the midst of the Church, this awesome revelation of the wonderful Son of God.

The Importance of What We See

What we hear is important. But more important is what we see. What you see actually motivates how you live. What you see is that which draws you on. Abraham saw a city. It is what he saw in the vision that became the great motivation of his life, and what we see determines how we live. If you have seen a world in disaster, a church in collapse, and opposition gathering like the dark storm clouds of a coming calamity, then you will live on the defensive. But if you have seen the glory of the Lamb, if you have seen His radiance filling the earth, if you have seen His Kingdom coming and the nations of this world becoming the Kingdom of our God and of His Christ, then you will live in triumph. You will live an overcoming life because what you have seen in the Spirit is more real to you than what you see in the natural.

I do not know about you, but I have seen something. I have seen something of the purpose of God. I have seen something of the splendor of Jesus. I have seen something of the triumph of His Kingdom. I have seen something of the glory of His Church. I cannot entertain a thought of disappointment. I am not just an optimist, although I guess if I had to come down on either side, that is the side I would fall on. I think I am a realist. I think I am a Biblicist. I think I have seen some reality in the things of God. I think I have seen the Lord. One glimpse of Him would answer all your problems. If people encountered the Christ that we meet in the Book of Revelation, the queue for the counseling room would vanish overnight.

When I am speaking to some people, I sometimes feel like saying, "If you had seen what I have seen you would not be like you are." If you have seen Jesus, you can never be the same again. This is what happened to John: "I heard, I turned, I saw, I fell! I fell at His feet as though I were dead." When is the last time you saw Jesus in such a way that it had that impact on your life? When is the last time you were so overawed by the presence of Jesus that your legs turned to jelly and you fell in a heap at His feet? That is where He needs to get us because that is where the victory begins. It is not in us flexing our muscles or rattling our sabers. It is in us falling at the feet of Jesus. This is what happens when John encounters Christ. He hears the word, he lines his life up with the word, and in lining his life up, he sees the glory of Jesus and, in seeing the glory of Jesus, he falls like a dead man at His feet. That is where victory is discovered. That is where overcoming abounds—not in our histrionics but in bringing our lives in absolute and total submission to the lordship of Jesus Christ. When John goes up into Heaven, he is going to discover that he is not alone because all the elders fall down before the Lamb and worship Him. It is the place of utter submission. I am like a dead man at the feet of Jesus. If Jesus had a church full of dead men and dead women, this church would win the world very quickly.

He Strengthens Our Frailty

Here is John dead and at the feet of Jesus, and Jesus does three very important things for John. These are three very important things He will do for us if we bring ourselves in total submission to His lordship. You see, this Kingdom into which we have come, this Kingdom about which the whole Book of Revelation speaks, is a very strange place. It is not like anywhere else in the universe. It is a peculiar Kingdom because in this Kingdom if you want to find your life you have to lose it. In this Kingdom, if you want to be great you have to become the servant of all. What a strange place! I do not know anywhere else like it on the planet, or in the

Heavens. John discovers his strength when he falls like a dead man at the feet of Jesus. This is the message to the churches—death is not the end, it is often the beginning.

It says that he fell at the feet of Jesus like a dead man, and then, "He placed His right hand on me" (Rev. 1:17). Jesus, by this act of immense grace, strengthens John in his frailty. John's strength has gone. This strong man who stood against the Roman Empire, who had resisted the authority of Caesar, who had refused to compromise with all the pressures of Asia upon him, sees Jesus and is dead. But Jesus reaches out His right hand. It is significant that He reaches out *this* hand because it is in this hand that He holds seven stars, which are, He tells us, the seven angels of the churches. I think this refers to those who are His servants and who minister. And I think part of the confirmation—that is what it is—is that this is the hand with which He touches John and imparts strength to His feeble servant. When we come to the end of ourselves, when we come to the abandoning of our own strength, it is Jesus who strengthens our frailty.

He Stills Our Fears

Not only does He strengthen our frailty, but He stills our fears. For He speaks to John and says, "Do not be afraid" (Rev. 1:17). I find it encouraging that this outstanding apostle of God knew what it was to be afraid. We sometimes want to project a macho image of ourselves, as if fear could not affect us. But the truth is that we are often afraid. There is nothing wrong with being afraid; it is part of what God has built into you. Fear gets the adrenalin going so that you either fight or flee. That is what fear does for you. That is what it is supposed to do. Fear throws us on the Lord. When Paul went to Corinth he said to the Corinthians that he came with "fear, and with much trembling"

(1 Cor. 2:3). He is not speaking about being under an anointing that caused physical trembling. He is scared. But he finds his strength in the Lord. God comes to this blessed apostle and says to him, "Do not be afraid." He stills our fears. When we have encountered Christ like this, there is nothing to scare us. When we have encountered Jesus like this, fear flees. The great hymn writers of old wrote songs of such great revelation and anthems of praise and worship that we have sadly assigned to yesteryear, and in doing so, we have thrown away some of our heritage that we need to rediscover. We need to rediscover the hymns of our fathers because they are full of truth much more than some of the ditties we sing today. One of these great writers wrote this: "Fear Him, ye saints, and then ye will nothing else fear." I like that. There is a dragon out there. There is a beast out there. There is a false prophet out there. There is a seductive harlot out there, but Jesus says to us, "Do not be afraid." He strengthens our weakness and he stills our fear.

He looks at John lying at His feet like a dead man, and as if to say, "I have been there. I know what it is like," He says, "I am the Living One; I was dead, and behold I am alive for ever and ever!" (Rev. 1:18). We are called to share in the strength and the security of His resurrection. If I know I am raised with Christ, then death no longer holds fear for me. It was by His death that Jesus destroyed him who has the power of death and released those who through fear of death were all their lives subject to bondage (Heb. 2:14-15). You do not have to be afraid of dying. The fear of death has left me. I am not looking forward to it. I would rather not be around when it happens! The pain that sometimes accompanies it does not fill me with delight. Death is still an enemy—but it is a toothless enemy. It is a clawless enemy. It is an unmasked fiend who, behind the wretched grimace, is just a clown who has been brought into the service of King Jesus. His job now only consists of opening the door for you into the presence of the Savior. He is a doorkeeper. That's all he is. We do not have anything to fear. Jesus wants us to know this.

He Secures Our Future

Jesus says, "Do not be afraid. I am the First and the Last. I am the Living One; I was dead, and behold I am alive for ever and ever! And I hold the keys of death and hades" (Rev. 1:17-18). Do you know why He has the keys of death and hell? He overcame him who once held them. When satan came around after Jesus beat him on the cross, he felt in every pocket. Maybe he searched under every cushion. And Jesus shouted, "I've got the keys! I've got the keys!" Do you know your future is secure because He has got the keys? You can overcome because He has got the keys. Satan does not have the key to your future. Satan does not have the key to your prison. If you feel you are in prison, get up and try the door. It's open! Jesus has the keys, and it is Jesus who is going to unlock everything from now on. Nothing is going to happen in the Book of Revelation from this moment onwards unless Jesus unlocks it and allows it to come forth. Satan has no strategy. All satan has is reactions. But the Lamb sets the agenda. The Lamb opens the seals. The Lamb unlocks the doors. The Lamb sets in motion His eternal purposes. This is the Christ who is our Lord. This is the Jesus who has conquered all things and now calls to us, "Overcome, overcome! Because I am alive, you are alive. Because I have won, you win. There are troubles but I have overcome the world and I invite you to join Me in My victory." That is why the Scripture says He always leads us in triumphal procession in Christ (2 Cor. 2:14). That is why Paul tells us we are more than conquerors through Him who loved us

(Rom. 8:37). We are called to win. There is no room in the Church of Jesus Christ for a ghetto mentality. There is no room for "pastor's last stand." We do not have to hold the fort. We have to invade the enemy's territory!

The Messages to the Churches

Jesus enables us to overcome. And every message that Jesus sends to the churches in chapters 2 and 3 is a call to overcome. It is interesting, and in some ways it is a bit of an embarrassing encouragement, to discover that those early churches had problems, difficulties, and errors. Jesus confronts them not just to blow them out but to bring them in line with His revealed purpose. As He calls them to overcome, it is interesting to note that some dispensationalists will tell us that these seven churches are a picture of the history of the church. It starts in the past with the Ephesian church, which was orthodox and did not have great error. Although it had lost its first love, it was orthodox, it was a good church. The last church, in the last dispensation before Jesus comes again, is Laodicea, a lukewarm church that God wants to spit out of His mouth. Dispensationalism always carries with it a sense of failure. It traces dispensations down through history and every one ends in failure. Even the Church is going to end in failure. I cannot embrace any concept that speaks of this people for whom Jesus died, this Church that He purchased at such inestimable cost, as ultimately failing and disappointing Him.

Now, I am not claiming right now that the Church is perfect. We are all aware that it is not. We know about our own churches—fulfilling as they may be, none of us would proclaim, "This is the pattern for everything that has to happen from now on." But we are trying to get there, and by God's grace we will succeed. One of

81

the things it is important to understand is that although He addresses each church individually, every church is included in the letter. He does not end the letters by saying, "Let him who has an ear to hear, hear what the Spirit is saying to Ephesus." It says, "Let him hear what the Spirit is saying to the churches." That is why I often say that if you are in a meeting and there is a prophetic word that comes to an individual and some of it, somehow, in the Spirit of God, wings its way into your heart, then that was for you. Imagine I am a believer in Pergamum and I'm reading the letter that went to Ephesus and something rings in my heart because it is for me. It is what the Spirit is saying to the churches. What is more, there does seem to be a recapitulation of spiritual history in these letters: there is no looking forward to degenerating faith but a recounting of progressive purposes.

Ephesus—Paradise Restored

The overcomers in Ephesus are promised access to the tree of life. God has begun His restoration purpose way back in the garden. Here is His purpose: paradise restored. You have been excluded from the garden. Sin has separated you from the tree of life—but if you overcome, you will have access to the tree of life. Paradise is restored.

Smyrna—Pardon Secured

To Smyrna He says that he who overcomes will not be hurt by the second death. The second death is not dying physically but dying spiritually. It is being cast eternally from the presence of God. It works like this. If you are born once you will die twice. You will die physically, but you will die eternally in a separation from God. If you are born twice you only die once. Those who overcome will not be hurt by the second death. In fact, Jesus says, "Be faithful, even to the point of death, and I will give you the crown of life" (Rev. 2:10). So the death that came on Adam when he sinned has now been removed, and Smyrna speaks to us of pardon secured.

Pergamum—Provision Supplied

The church in Pergamum is on a pilgrimage. It is as though they are going through the wilderness now toward their final destination. To him that overcomes God promises hidden manna, just as Israel fed on manna in the wilderness. God promises to provide everything that we need. Pergamum and the overcomers there are promised that their provision will be supplied, that God will give them all that they need to sustain them in their pilgrimage until they come to the land of promise.

Thyatira—Power Delegated

To Thyatira He says that He will give them authority over the nations if they overcome. Just as Israel came out of the wilderness into the land and overcame all the nations that dwelt there, so the Church in the world is to overcome all the nations and bring in the Kingdom of God. His power will be delegated to those who overcome.

Sardis—Priesthood Established

To Sardis He says that those who overcome will be given white garments. They are going to be dressed like priests, for in God's ongoing purpose He will establish the priesthood of His people dressed in white that they might minister to Him, their names written in His book. It is interesting that when Nehemiah came back to rebuild the walls and the people sought to discover who were priests and who were Levites, there was some confusion after 70 years of neglect and of forgetfulness. One family came forward and said they were priests, but they could not find their names in the book. Because their names were not in the book they were considered as unclean. But if your name is in the book, then you are clean. You have a white robe, and He establishes you in His priesthood to minister before Him forever.

Philadelphia—Permanence Promised

To Philadelphia He says that those who overcome will become pillars in the temple. He is building the temple now. We have left the tabernacle behind. We are building a temple for the glory of God, one in which He will dwell and manifest His presence and speak to the nations. You and I will be pillars in His temple. We will be unmovable, unshakable. We will have a sense of permanence in the purposes of God. James and John were pillars in the church.

When Solomon built the temple, he put in two bronze pillars. They had nothing to do with the structure. They did not hold it up. They did not support anything. They just stood at the entrance of the temple, two huge bronze pillars. He gave them names. One was called Jakin and the other was called Boaz. Jakin means "He establishes." Boaz means "in Him is strength." You and I are pillars established and strengthened by God in the house of the Lord. This is the promise to all those who overcome.

Laodicea—Partnership Offered

To Laodicea, there is a strange promise to this lukewarm, failing, deceived church; deceived not by some satanic infiltration but in their own thinking, in their own boasting and pride. He tells them that if they overcome, they will sit down with Him on His throne just as He overcame and sat down with the Father on His throne. So He takes us from the garden to the throne, through the wilderness to the temple. He takes us through the priesthood and says that all this is for those who will overcome. Of course, the good news is this: you can overcome.

Born to Overcome

Let me show you an interesting short passage in chapter 17 of Revelation,

> *"The ten horns you saw are ten kings who have not yet received a kingdom, but who for one hour will receive authority as kings along with the beast. They have one purpose and will give their power and authority to the beast. They will make war against the Lamb, but the Lamb will overcome them because He is Lord of lords and King of kings—and with Him will be His called, chosen and faithful followers"* (Revelation 17:12-14).

It's great isn't it? There are so many people majoring on the beast, the ten kings, the horns, the war, the invasion, the terror—and with one almost-throwaway line, John casts it aside like so much rubbish. The Lamb will overcome them. We are not told how He does it. We are not told what His strategy is. We are not given the details of the war. We are not in the cabinet meeting to hear the discussion as to exactly how they are going to stand against this terrible invasion, this great axis of evil. He just says that the Lamb will overcome. Why? Because He is King of kings and Lord of lords! And do you know what? He still is—and He is *our* King and *our* Lord, and He always leads us in triumphal procession in Christ Jesus. He is the overcomer. To the Laodiceans He says that he who overcomes will sit with Him on His throne just as He overcame.

We do not have to work at overcoming. We just have to line ourselves up with Jesus. We just have to be able to say with Paul,

"I have been crucified with Christ and I no longer live, but Christ lives in me. The life I live in the body, I live by faith in the Son of God, who loved me and gave himself for me" (Galatians 2:20).

You and I were born again to overcome. Jesus never invested in a loser. He took multitudes of losers, but He turned them into winners. He took multitudes of those who were defeated and transformed them into conquerors. He is saying to a people who were facing far more tribulation than you and I will probably meet in a lifetime, He is writing to people who are under the threat of imprisonment, to people who are under the threat of persecution, who are under the threat of death, and He is saying to them, "You can overcome! You can overcome!" We can win, and the reason, the guarantee, the certainty of our overcoming is that He has overcome. His resurrection is the guarantee of our victory.

Speaking of the antichrist, John says, in his first letter, "You, dear children, are from God and have overcome them, because the one who is in you is greater than the one who is in the world" (1 John 4:4). By the way, the Book of Revelation never uses the word *antichrist*. It is not a word that you find there. John does use it in his letter, but he doesn't identify it as a person. He identifies it as a spirit. The spirit of antichrist is anything and everything that is opposed to Jesus. There is a spirit of antichrist out there. It shows itself in many ways. It shows itself in Islam and in Humanism. It shows itself in immoral behavior and in binding legalism. We do not have to ask where the spirit of antichrist is. It is everywhere Christ is not. It is everywhere you are not. There is a spirit of antichrist at work out there, but that doesn't have to frighten us. It doesn't have to cause us to worry or bring anxiety because, as John tells us, the one who is in us is greater than the one in the world. We have overcome. We have all the equipment we need to overcome. We have all the power we need to overcome. We have all the authority we need to overcome. What is that equipment, that power, that authority? The one who is in you. Who is in you? Christ is in you, the hope of glory (Col. 1:27).

There is no excuse for failure here. There is no excuse for capitulation here. The apostle John states, "Everyone born of God overcomes the world" (1 John 5:4). That is a very bold statement, an amazing claim. Everyone born of God overcomes the world. We have to struggle sometimes with what we perceive is reality and what we believe is the Word of God. If you have ever sat down and counseled people, they will tell you this: "That is just the way I am." No, it is not! They are living a lie if they are living in failure, in fear, in depression. They are living a lie. That is not the truth. It is a deception. The truth is this: everyone born of God overcomes the world. That is the truth.

Now if my experience is not matching up to the truth, I have to change my experience, not the truth. I need to learn to know and confess who I am in Christ. I see Jesus not just to make me feel even smaller, but I see Jesus so that I can begin to understand who I am in Christ and begin to confess the truth. This is the truth: everyone born of God overcomes the world. Have I been born of God? Yes. I have been born of the Spirit. It happened to me many years ago. I remember the moment. It was a divine drama acted out in the quietness of my own room. It was an encounter with God that revolutionized my life from that moment on and has been more radically revolutionizing my life since. Something happened. I was born again. I was born of God.

I was born from above. Do you know what that means? I can overcome the world. This is not boasting. Or if it is, it is boasting in the Lord. It is confessing the truth. What did Joel say? Not only did He say, "Afterward, I will pour out My Spirit," He also said, "Let the weakling say, 'I am strong!'" (Joel 3:10). Why? Are you just psyching yourself up? Is it just hype? No, no—that is the truth. You may feel weak, but the reality is you are strong. If you just confess what you are, you are halfway to fulfilling what God has for you. "Everyone born of God overcomes the world. This is the victory that has overcome the world, even our faith. Who is it that overcomes the world? Only he who believes that Jesus is the Son of God" (1 John 5:4-5).

Who is it that overcomes the world? The super saint? The faith preacher? The apostles? No, he who believes that Jesus is the Son of God! I can do that. I can manage that! I do not have to do super-saint spiritual sit-ups. I can believe that Jesus is the Son of God. I do believe it. I believe it with all my heart. I believe it without question. I believe it without any hint of compromise. I believe with all the conviction and certainty of my heart that Jesus is the Son of God. He is the Christ, the Son of the living God. Well then, I can be blessed because Jesus says that it is on such a confession that He will build His church and the gates of hell shall not overcome it, shall not prevail against it (Matt. 16:13-20). What does that mean? It means I am going to overcome the gates of hell. We are all overcomers, not because of something we have achieved but because of something we have believed and someone we have believed in.

In the twelfth chapter of Revelation we see the old serpent being cast down from Heaven. We see the dragon hurled to the ground. We see his tail sweeping away a third of the stars. He has lost his place of authority. He has lost his place of influence. He has been cast down to the ground. He is the one who every time you believed you were a failure came along and confirmed it by speaking it into your spirit. He is the accuser of the brothers, but he has been cast down. He is the accuser of the brethren, but he has been hurled out of the Heavens. And, says John, they—that is, the brothers, the saints, the believers, the church—they overcame him by the blood of the Lamb. You see, it is not a magic formula, the blood of the Lamb. It is not something we recite, "The blood, the blood, the blood." The blood of the Lamb just means we take a firm stand in our identification with Him who was crucified. His blood was shed for me.

They overcame him by the blood of the Lamb and the word of their testimony. It is not that they stood in front of satan and said, "In August 1960 I gave my life to Jesus." That is not the word of your testimony. The word of your testimony is this: "I am a child of God." The word of your testimony is, in the words of an old hymn, "I have an interest in the bleeding lamb." He died for me. You can accuse however much you like. You can write a list as long as a roll of wallpaper with all the things about me, with everything that you have found out, everything that you have discovered, everything that you have invented and made me believe. You can write a list as long as you like, but Jesus took hold of that list and He nailed it to the cross and it is gone.

Maybe, who knows, there are some of you reading this now who will seal your testimony with your blood. Do not be surprised. There are brothers and sisters, hundreds and thousands of them, who are doing that very thing today. Satan can kill us, but he cannot beat us. He can persecute us, but he cannot overcome us. Why? Because Jesus lives, I will live. Because Jesus has over-come, I will overcome. Because He has sat down on the throne, I will sit with Him on His throne. I am called to conquer. I am chosen to overcome, not because there is something special about me, but because of this one thing: He set His affection on me. He shed His blood for me. He has included me in His great salvation, and satan cannot touch me at all.

CHAPTER 5

The Four Horsemen

At the beginning of this chapter it will be a great benefit to remind ourselves of the Scriptures by reading Revelation 5:1-7 and 6:1-8, where we find the Lamb opening the scroll and the emergence of the four horsemen. These four horsemen have been the focus of all kind of fantasies, dramas, and artistic representations, and they are usually seen as horrific harbingers of dreadful times to come. In a measure, that is true. But what we need to understand is that these things are released not from the pit, but from Heaven. These things are called forth not by demonic powers, but by the four cherubim that surround the throne of God. "Come!" they cry, and as they cry, the horse comes forth to fulfill everything that God has ordained. We need to understand that it is the Lamb who is breaking the seals. This is not some fiendish satanic plot that is being set into motion. This is the Lamb, the governor of all history, fulfilling His plan and His purpose.

The best commentary that you will ever find on the Bible is the Bible. The Bible explains itself. That is what it is designed to do. We compare Scripture with Scripture. The things that we say, believe, and act upon must be confirmed by the Word of God—not just by one verse taken out of context, but by the whole weight of Scripture. Somebody once said that a text out of context is a pretext. That is very true. We do not just take a snippet here and a snippet there. We seek to weigh the whole counsel of God so that we can come to an understanding of the truth. God did not write the Bible to confuse us. God had the Bible communicated to us that we might see and understand. That has always been my approach to the Word of God, as it should be for us all. What I want to try to do is to throw new light on these horses and their riders and ultimately on the purposes of God. I want to do this so that we are not those that live in fear and dread of the day when the dark clouds of the sky suddenly transform into some dreadful and fearsome quartet riding out to do us harm. Rather, we see this as part and parcel of the ongoing purposes of God.

An Equestrian Vision

The whole idea of horsemen riding forth finds its genesis in the Book of Zechariah. Zechariah is a young prophet who, significantly, has returned from Babylonian captivity. He has been a captive in Babylon. He has returned with Zerubbabel the prince and with Joshua the priest, and he has returned to Jerusalem with the specific task of building the house of God. Nehemiah will come later to build the walls of the city, but the first wave of returnees out of captivity came just to build the house. When

Zechariah, who is a priest as well as a prophet, gets his visions from God, he gets eight visions in one night—a fairly busy period of revelation. Most of his visions are to do with the house of God. He sees the visions in the context of the temple that they have come back to build. Let us turn back to Zechariah:

> *On the twenty-fourth day of the eleventh month, the month of Shebat, in the second year of Darius, the word of the Lord came to the prophet Zechariah son of Berekiah, the son of Iddo. During the night I had a vision—and there before me was a man riding a red horse! He was standing among the myrtle trees in a ravine. Behind him were red, brown and white horses. I asked, "What are these, my lord?" The angel who was talking with me answered, "I will show you what they are." Then the man standing among the myrtle trees explained, "They are the ones the Lord has sent to go throughout the earth." And they reported to the angel of the Lord, who was standing among the myrtle trees, "We have gone throughout the earth and found the whole world at rest and in peace"* (Zechariah 1:7-11).

They are the messengers of God, another picture of the angels who go forth. These horsemen represent angelic messengers who serve the purposes of God. In chapter 6 of the prophet Zechariah we find another equestrian vision:

> *I looked up again—and there before me were four chariots coming out from between two mountains—mountains of bronze!* (Zechariah 6: 1)

In an earlier chapter, I wrote of the two bronze pillars that stood at the doorway of the temple. So these chariots are coming out from the house of God. They are coming from the temple, past the two bronze pillars, past the two bronze mountains:

> *The first chariot had red horses, the second black, the third white, and the fourth dappled—all of them powerful....*
> *When the powerful horses went out, they were straining to go throughout the earth. And he said, "Go throughout the earth!" So they went throughout the earth. Then he called to me, "Look, those going toward the north country have given my Spirit rest in the land of the north"* (Zechariah 6:2-3; 7-8).

Note that the ultimate goal of the horsemen is to bring peace and rest. Their ultimate goal is to bring in the qualities of the Kingdom of God. For the quality of the Kingdom of God is not eating and drinking, it is not rule and regulation, it's not diet and day observation; the Kingdom of God is righteousness, peace, and joy in the Holy Spirit (Rom. 14:17). Everything God does is geared to bringing in His Kingdom. Even the judgments of God, things that appear to be destructive from the hand of God, actually have a creative conclusion. God wants to bring in His Kingdom. So these angelic messengers are not just harbingers of destruction and calamity. They are messengers of the Kingdom. God wants to bring in His Kingdom. He wants to establish peace and rest among His people.

The White Horse—The Conquering King

John is watching as the Lamb takes the book and opens the seal. The first horse out of the stable, the first horse that gallops throughout the world, is described like this: a white horse, its rider holding a bow and given a crown as He rode out as a conqueror bent on conquest. When God initiates His purpose, the first one out is none other than Jesus Himself. Now this is when human logic begins to get into conflict with spiritual understanding. How can the Lamb open the book and let Himself out? How can it be that the Lamb opens the seal and then it is Jesus who rides out on the horse? It is illogical. Well, let me give you a very simple example. When He began His earthly ministry, when He announced His intention, Jesus went into the synagogue. He was handed a scroll, the scroll of the prophet Isaiah.

> *Unrolling it, He found the place where it is written: "The Spirit of the Lord is on me, because he has anointed Me to preach good news to the poor. He has sent Me to proclaim freedom for the prisoners and recovery of sight for the blind, to release the oppressed, to proclaim the year of the Lord's favor."...The eyes of everyone in the synagogue were fastened on Him, and He began by saying to them, "Today this scripture is fulfilled in your hearing"* (Luke 4:18-21).

Do you see what happened? Jesus took the scroll, opened the scroll, and introduced Himself out of the scroll. Now in Revelation we are seeing Him in a different dimension; we see Him not as the carpenter in a local synagogue but as the Lamb, the center of all Heaven. And yet He is still doing the same thing. He is taking the scroll, opening the scroll, and introducing Himself. He Himself gallops out of the scroll to fulfill the purposes of God.

All the way through the Book of Revelation white represents purity and holiness, and so the Lamb comes forth riding on a white horse. The first thing that God does when He wants to produce His purposes in the world is to declare His Word, to preach His Gospel. Everything depends on how we respond to the Word of God. We are going to see this rider later on in chapter 19, when there is no question about who He is. He is coming out riding on a horse, and His name is the Word of God. The Word of God is the first thing that God looses into the world to judge and discriminate. This is how it works. Right at the beginning of creation, "God said." God's word comes into play. "And God said, 'Let there be light,' and there was light." And "God saw that the light was good, and He separated the light from the darkness" (Gen. 1:3-4). That is how God operates. God says, God sees, and then God separates. What we will find in the Book of Revelation is that the Word of God goes out, God sees those who have responded and become light and those who have rejected and becomes darkness, and then God separates them.

Now the Lamb is riding forth as the Word of God, and He has a crown because He is King of kings and Lord of lords. In fact, in chapter 19 we will see Him riding out with many crowns on His head, and the name written on His thigh and on His robe is "King of kings and Lord of lords." He is riding forth as a conqueror. He is not going to *become* a conqueror. He *is* a conqueror. Before He has unsheathed His mighty sword, before He has strung His powerful bow, He is already a conqueror. And as a conqueror He rides forth bent on conquest, determined to overcome, determined to win, determined to bring in the Kingdom. It is the saints and Jesus who are overcomers. It is the saints and Jesus who ride on white horses. It is the saints and Jesus who wear crowns.

The last chapter of the prophet Habakkuk is a song. It is a worship song, a celebration. It is a harmonious prophecy. What the prophet is doing is recounting the historic demonstrations of God's power. He takes from different periods of history, from different victories, different times of God manifesting His power, and weaves it all together in one splendid declaration of the triumphs of the Lord. We have pictures of God taking His people through the sea, of Joshua making the sun stand still in the sky, of David slaying Goliath. All kinds of things come together in one composite picture of the greatness of God. One of the things the prophet says is, "God we have heard of your deeds, we stand in awe of what you have done. Repeat them. Renew them in our day." One of the great things for us is to know that what God has done in the past, God determines to do again in the future. The great things God has done in the past are hints and clues to us of what God yet wants to do in the days to come. So the prophet asks God to renew these things in his day, and he begins to compose a song that weaves in all kinds of demonstrations of God's power. Bearing in mind these four horsemen have ridden out, see how Habakkuk rejoices in the power and the glory of God.

Psalm 45 is a great Psalm. We will give it fuller treatment when we get to chapter 19, but let us note here that it is about a war and a wedding. The strange thing is that, in the purposes of God, a war and a wedding are often placed together. Chapter 19 of Revelation and Psalm 45 are examples of those war-wedding pictures. The great King is riding forth: "Gird Your sword upon Your side, O mighty one; clothe Yourself with splendor and majesty." The great King is bringing in the qualities of the Kingdom, "In Your majesty ride forth victoriously in behalf of truth, humility and righteousness." He has His sword at His side and His bow in His hand, and His arrows are sharp and they are going to penetrate the hearts of His enemies: "Let your right hand display awesome deeds. Let your sharp arrows pierce the hearts of the king's enemies; let the nations fall beneath your feet." What we are seeing here in Revelation has already been prophesied in Psalm 45.

Lord, I have heard of your fame; I stand in awe of your deeds, O Lord. Renew them in our day, in our time make them known; in wrath remember mercy (Habakkuk 3:2).

"In wrath remember mercy" is a good motto for the Book of Revelation because there is going to be a lot of wrath breaking forth; but in His wrath, God always remembers mercy: Here is God going forth, and as we read it we are going to discover that God goes forth as a Redeemer, as a Savior. He rides out as one who will rescue His people. But as He rides out, pestilence and plague accompany Him: "Plague went before Him; pestilence followed His steps" (Hab. 3:5). It should not surprise us, therefore, when we look into the Book of Revelation and see Jesus riding out to conquer the world, that plague and pestilence are with Him, because that is one of the ways that the prophets describe the purposes of God coming to fulfillment.

The Red Horse—The Sword of Separation

One of the things we see as these horsemen ride forth is in His wake comes war, famine, pestilence, and death. That is just how the prophet in this third chapter of Habakkuk describes Him. This is none other than the Lord riding out triumphantly, and our emphasis is on His triumph, not on the repercussions that follow the rejection of His lordship. Nevertheless, there are repercussions. For the next horse that comes forth, we are told, is a red horse. In fact, it is a fiery red horse. Its rider was given power to take peace from the earth and to make men slay each other. To him was given a large sword. Do you remember those words of Jesus, "Do not suppose that I have come to bring peace to the earth. I did not come to bring peace, but a sword" (Matt. 10:34)? You see, when Jesus rides out in triumph, there are those who bow the knee to His lordship and those who reject His offer of salvation; and God separates them just as a shepherd separates the sheep from the goats. Wherever the Gospel is preached, there is inevitably a violent reaction. In fact, if we read on in Matthew after the verse just quoted about the sword, Jesus says that a man's enemy shall be that of his own household: father against son, mother against daughter. There is a division that comes between those who believe and those who reject the Gospel. Sometimes the opposition that arises between them involves violence. There are nations in the world right now where people who dare to believe on the Lord Jesus Christ could be murdered by their own family simply because they have owned the name of Jesus. These are the things that follow in the wake of the Gospel. These are inevitable repercussions that happen everywhere that the Gospel is proclaimed and everywhere that Jesus establishes His rule. There are those who rebel and are violent in their rebellion. And so Jesus brings in the Kingdom, but, in doing so, He brings a sword.

The Black Horse—Famine and Finance

He opens the third seal and there comes a black horse whose rider is holding a pair of scales and saying that the minimum subsistence will cost a whole day's wage. There is famine coming. You see, this world is God's world, and everything that happens in this world serves the purpose of God. Where there are those who do not respond to the Gospel, there is an economic effect. We sometimes divorce spiritual things from natural things. The Bible has no concept of that at all. As far as the Bible is concerned, everything is spiritual because everything issues from God. Your economic situation is a spiritual thing. It is not just a natural thing. That is why the Bible makes it very clear that God wants us to prosper. That is why the Bible makes it clear that he who sows much will reap much. Where there is a society that rejects God, there is a society that will come under financial pressure. It may not happen immediately, but somewhere down the line it will happen. It will happen because righteousness exalts a nation but sin is a reproach to any people (Prov. 14:34). God begins to touch us, and we will see in the Book of Revelation that one of the ways God begins to touch things is economically.

So there is a sense of famine that comes. It may be a real famine, a shortage of supply, or it may be a famine of hearing the Word of God, for the Scripture speaks of that also. But while a rejecting world is suffering in the areas of its economy, God makes a promise to His people. Listen to what it says here: "A quart of wheat for a day's wages, and three quarts of barley for a day's wages, and do not damage the oil and the wine!" (Rev. 6:6). Now some interpreters see this as the poor suffering because staple things are scarce and the rich prospering because expensive things are plentiful. But when we look into the Scriptures, we discover that oil and wine actually have deep implications for us. It is one of the ways God describes His people.

Back in the Book of Judges when Abimelech had killed all of Gideon's sons and set himself up as king over the people of God, the youngest son, called Jotham, escaped. As Abimelech was trying to set himself as a king to the leaders of the nation, Jotham went up on a mountain and shouted a parable down. "Let me tell you a story," he said.

> *"All the trees were looking for a king and they said to the olive tree, 'Come and be our king,' and the olive tree said, 'Shall I leave my oil that blesses God and men to be your king?' So they said to the vine, 'Come and be our king,' and the vine said, 'Should I leave my wine that gladdens the*

*heart of men and come and be your king?' and he would
not. In the end, they submitted themselves to the thorn
bush, the very mark of the curse of the earth, and he became their king and ruled over them"* (Judges 9:8-15).

Now what we see here is that the olive tree and the vine actually join God and men together. When you come into the
New Testament, it is very interesting that Paul speaks of believers as branches being grafted into an olive tree (Rom. 11:17).
And Jesus says He is the vine and we are the branches (John
15:4-5). There is a relationship, an intimacy, between God and
men. There is a relationship between Jesus and us. We are
branches of His olive tree. We are branches of His vine. The
olive tree and the vine represent the people of God. The
psalmist says of God's provision that He gives wine to make
our heart glad and oil to make our faces shine (Ps. 104:15). The
wine of the Kingdom makes us glad, and the oil of the Spirit
causes us to glow. We are God's olive and vine people. If your
name was Olive Vine, that would be fantastic, wouldn't it! You
would be a personification of our relationship with God. In
fact, when we come together, as the Church of Christ, wine and
oil play an important part in our fellowship. We drink wine to
remember Him, and we anoint with oil to receive His healing.
Oil and wine have a special implication for you and me as
God's people.

So when this angelic creature is given authority to bring
famine into the world, he touches everything except you and
me. He touches everything except the olive and the vine. One of
the things we need to understand in the Book of Revelation is
that when all these plagues and perils break out on the earth,
horrendous and wretched as they are, they do not touch us. One

of the things we will see as we look later at the Exodus paradigm is how much John lifts from the Exodus story and applies it to us. One of the great things about the plagues that came on Egypt is that they did not come on the people of God. They came everywhere except the camp of the Lord. Now you and I need to know that whatever breaks out on this earth, we are safe. "Do not touch the oil and the wine." You can burn the grass. You can cut down the forest. You can turn the water to blood, but you cannot touch the olive and the vine because they are the trees that fill the garden of God. These are the redeemed and the preserved of the Lord, upon whom He has set His affection.

Let me just refer here briefly to the seven trumpets and the seven plagues. In chapter 9 of Revelation, we are told of the trumpets being blown, and when they are blown, all kinds of calamities hit our world.

> *The fifth angel sounded his trumpet, and I saw a star that had fallen from the sky to the earth. The star was given the key to the shaft of the Abyss. When he opened the Abyss, smoke rose from it like the smoke from a gigantic furnace. The sun and sky were darkened by the smoke from the Abyss. And out of the smoke locusts came down upon the earth and were given power like that of scorpions of the earth. They were told not to harm the grass of the earth or any plant or tree, but only those people who did not have the seal of God on their foreheads* (Revelation 9:1-4).

You see, when all hell breaks out, you and I can still live in Heaven on earth. When they are plaguing the rest of mankind, when the whole world is suffering because of its rejection of Christ and its rebellion against the Gospel, God says to those agents of suffering, "You are still on My leash; you can only do what I allow you to do. Do not touch the grass." It's funny because the very thing that locusts want is the grass and the trees. But God says not to touch them. Why? Because they represent God's people; the righteous spring up like grass, they are oaks of righteousness, the planting of the Lord. The only ones the locusts can touch are those who do not have the seal of God on their forehead. How do you know that you are sealed? You have His name upon your forehead.

In chapter 16 of Revelation, it speaks of the bowls of wrath that are poured out on our world:

> *The first angel went and poured out his bowl on the land, and ugly and painful sores broke out on the people who had the mark of the beast and worshiped his image* (Revelation 16:2).

There are two kinds of people in our world. We are not talking about future world; we are talking about today's world. There are two kinds of people in this world. There are those who have the mark of God on them and those who have the mark of the beast on them. It is not your VISA card; it is not a barcode. There is a mark of God on all those who name the name of Jesus, and there is a mark of the beast on all those who have not received the Gospel. The Bible makes it very clear; the locusts cannot touch those who have the mark of God. They can only torment and plague those who have the mark of the beast. Whichever way it falls, we are safe.

Now, that does not mean we do not get touched by pain, that we escape on some kind of cloud and look at the world through rose-colored glasses. We get persecuted. We may get martyred.

God preserves us, even if that preservation takes us through death and brings us into His presence.

The Green Horse—Rejection and Repercussions

The last of the horses that comes forth, the Bible tells us, is a pale horse or, probably more accurately, a green horse, which is very bizarre. But its very color, its very pallor, speaks of sickness, plague, and pestilence. We should note that the first fulfillment of these judgments was on Jerusalem. It was Jerusalem that had rejected the Gospel of Christ. It was Jerusalem that had refused His kingship. It was Jerusalem that claimed they had no king but Caesar. It was Jerusalem that had crucified the Lord of Glory. And in their rejection of the covenant, God therefore rejected them. And many things that happen in the Book of Revelation are warnings that God gave Israel in the Old Testament. It is Israel that had the warning. It is Israel that becomes the prostitute. It is Israel that has become Babylon. It is Israel that has rejected Him, and it is upon Israel that terrible plagues and pestilences are initially poured out. It happened dramatically in A.D. 70, when the Romans destroyed the city and scattered the Jews to the ends of the earth. But the warning actually comes way back in Leviticus:

> But if you will not listen to Me and carry out all these commands, and if you reject My decrees and abhor My laws and fail to carry out all My commands and so violate My covenant, then I will do this to you: I will bring upon you sudden terror, wasting diseases and fever that will destroy your sight and drain away your life. You will plant seed in vain, because your enemies will eat it. I will set My face against you so that you will be defeated by your enemies; those who hate you will rule over you, and you will flee even when no one is pursuing you. If after all this you will

not listen to Me, I will punish you for your sins seven times over (Leviticus 26:14-18).

This passage in Leviticus 26 goes on to repeat its warning of punishment seven times, and the same seven-fold pattern unfolds in the Book of Revelation.

> *If you remain hostile toward Me and refuse to listen to Me, I will multiply your afflictions seven times over, as your sins deserve. I will send wild animals against you, and they will rob you of your children, destroy your cattle and make you so few in number that your roads will be deserted* (Leviticus 26:21-22).

Again and again, God says that there is a sevenfold judgment coming, and the sevenfold judgment has four characteristics. The four characteristics are the sword, famine, plague, and wild animals, which are the very plagues that this last horseman brings forth. He is called death, and hades is following him. But remember, Jesus said that He has the keys of death and hades. This horse can only ride forth because Jesus has unlocked the stable. Jesus is still in charge.

So God's prime purpose is for His Gospel to go forth and for all men to repent. But where there is no repentance, man sets in motion inevitable repercussions. There come hostility and violence, famine, pestilence, and death. But that is not God's initial purpose. He will destroy His enemies, but His desire is that all come to repentance. That is why the Gospel goes forth first. That is why He is the first one out of the stable, to declare the great things of God.

God is about to release the four horsemen on the earth. But before that happens, it is as if a cry goes up: "Hold your horses!

Hold your horses!" Something has to happen first. Remember, the Book of Revelation is not chronological. It is looking at things from different angles. So John sees the four horses released, he sees what is going to happen, but before that happens, a cry goes up, "hold your horses, hold back those four spirits, because something must happen first." We will look and see what that something is in our next chapter.

CHAPTER 6

Sealed and Delivered

We saw in the last chapter that before anything is released to achieve the purpose of God, there is a cry that goes up: "Hold your horses!" In chapter 7 this pause is pictured for us in another way:

> *After this I saw four angels standing at the four corners of the earth, holding back the four winds of the earth to prevent any wind from blowing on the land or on the sea or on any tree* (Revelation 7:1).

The angels that are spoken of back in Zechariah are also called the four winds, and they are held back now until God does something of extreme importance. This is what happens.

> *Then I saw another angel coming up from the east, having the seal of the living God. He called out in a loud voice to*

*the four angels who had been given power to harm the land
and the sea: "Do not harm the land or the sea or the trees
until we put a seal on the foreheads of the servants of our
God." Then I heard the number of those who were sealed:
144,000 from all the tribes of Israel* (Revelation 7:2-4).

The True Israel

Now this is another one of those happy hunting grounds for
all kinds of speculation. This is the ground upon which many
people believe that the Church will be removed and ethnic
Israel will do the job of bringing in the Kingdom of God. But if
we take time to read the letters to the seven churches in detail,
we find that one of the churches is persecuted by a group of
people who say they are Jews but are not (Rev. 2:9). He also
refers to these as the synagogue of satan (Rev. 2:9; 3:9). Ethnic
Israel rejected Jesus, and ethnic Israel took upon itself the
curses of covenant breaking. Ethnic Israel is not God's answer.
So what are we seeing here? Well, the New Testament tells us
very clearly that not all who claim to be Jews are Jews. Not all
who are descended physically from Abraham are true Israel,
Abraham's children (Rom. 9:6).

Jesus Himself said to the Jewish leaders of His generation
that they were of their father the devil (John 8:44). That is a
pretty drastic statement. He is a Jew, says Paul, not who is one
outwardly but who is one inwardly (Rom. 2:28-29). The church
is the true Israel of God. We are the "the circumcision, we who
worship by the Spirit of God" (Phil. 3:3). There has always been
a true Israel of God down through the Old Testament. Not
every ethnic Jew was a true child of God. Not every ethnic Jew,
at any time through history, was the real Israel. The real Israel
were those who were not just circumcised in the flesh but

circumcised in their hearts, those who obeyed the Lord, those who followed the Lord. The biblical term for it usually in the Old Testament is "a remnant." When the whole of the nation was moving toward apostasy, there was a faithful remnant: "Then those who feared the Lord talked with each other, and the Lord listened and heard. A scroll of remembrance was written in His presence concerning those who feared the Lord and honored His name" (Mal. 3:16). The true Israel always present in the Old Testament comes into finer definition in the New. Jesus described His disciples at one time as "the little flock"—that is, those who were the remnant of the true Israel (Luke 12:32) and who became the foundation of the Israel of God that was destined to fill the whole earth. You and I are God's spiritual Israel. We are children of promise and children born by the power of the Holy Spirit (see Gal. 4:28-29). So when we have this roll call of Israel here in chapter 7, we do not need to be worrying whether this is ethnic Israel. This is the true Israel of God.

God's Military Muster

The number twelve is significant, as we have also previously mentioned. It is the number of God's government, or God's Kingdom. It is used to describe those who belong to God, who live under the rule of God. Later on, when we look at the Heavenly city, we will see everything about it is in multiples of twelve. That is why Bible translators do us a disservice when they change it into meters or miles. That's not the point. We are not to see *how big* it is, but rather to understand *what* it is. And it is not to tell us actually *how many* there are; it is to tell us *who* they are. Twelve times twelve is one hundred and forty-four, which is then multiplied by one thousand to represent the completeness of all the redeemed people of God: 144,000.

This passage is actually a military muster. You may recall those passages in the Old Testament when God calls His people to war, taking a census of the people in order that the leadership will know what their military strength is. They are always mustered in thousands. Their military formations were in thousands. There are many references to the thousands of Israel. That is how they were recognized. That is how they were numbered. God's people were recorded in thousands and mustered under leaders of thousands. God is calling His people together for war. When we look at the second half of the chapter, we see that great multitude that nobody can number standing in the presence of God; it is the same people, but now they are at worship. God sees us differently when we are at war and when we are at worship. The church militant is God's thousands, ready, as we see later in chapter 14, to follow the Lamb wherever He goes. But the church at worship is represented as this innumerable multitude dressed in white and standing before the throne of God. So, this is a military muster.

A Living Seal

They are sealed with the seal of the living God. Now, that is interesting for this reason: because He is the living God, they are sealed with a living seal. When the writer to the Hebrews is talking about the Scriptures, he says, "The word of God is living and active" (Heb. 4:12). Therefore, when we read the Word of God, it should produce life and action because it is a living and active word. When we are sealed with the seal of the living God, it produces life in us because God is the living God. Now, the other thing we need to take note of is that when we meet this company again in chapter 14, it is immediately after the passage that deals with the beast and the mark of the beast. The mark of the beast is just a satanic, knee-jerk reaction to the mark of God. Satan did not invent this. He did not come up with the good idea to put a mark on all the wicked ones. God puts a mark on His people, and satan has a knee-jerk reaction because he has no creativity in him at all. He is not an initiator, just an imitator. When God does something, satan reacts. God seals His people so satan goes and seals his people. But God seals His people first. It is His idea. It is His initiative.

A Mark of Ownership

What does it mean when it says that He seals them? We find a company of people with Jesus' name or the Lamb's name written on their foreheads. They are marked as His property. I am a bibliophile. I love books. I love holding books. I love smelling books. I love reading books. I love books! And every book I have has a label stuck in the front. It says, "From the library of Tony Ling." They have a mark of ownership on them. Now you too have a mark of ownership on you. You belong to God.

A Mark of Preservation

Let me say a little about this mark that is on every true child of God. The first time we encounter God putting a mark on anybody is actually not in a good situation. Cain has murdered his brother and has been sent from the presence of the Lord. His fear is that if he leaves the presence of the Lord, anyone who finds him will kill him. And so to preserve Cain's life, God puts a visible mark on him. Although he is a wicked man, an evil and rebellious man, God, for His own reasons, wants to preserve his life and to do so puts a mark on him. The first time we encounter God putting a mark on anybody is for this specific reason—that his life will be spared. That helps us to understand what the mark of God on us will do. It will keep us safe. The mark of God will spare our life. The mark of God will keep us from being killed by the enemy. I do not mean it will prevent martyrdom. I hope we have already established that. But it is a mark of preservation. It is a mark that says, "We belong to God."

Now that picture in Revelation 7 actually comes from the Book of Ezekiel. In Ezekiel it is God coming to judge Israel. It is God bringing justice where there has been rebellion. In chapter 9 of Ezekiel, when Israel is in Babylonian captivity, the prophet goes back to Jerusalem, in the Spirit, and sees what God is up to in judging the people who still remain in the city:

> Then I heard Him call out in a loud voice, "Bring the guards of the city here, each with a weapon in his hand." And I saw six men coming from the direction of the upper gate, which faces north, each with a deadly weapon in his hand. With them was a man clothed in linen who had a writing kit at his side. They came in and stood beside the bronze altar. Now the glory of the God of Israel went up from above the cherubim, where it had been, and moved to the threshold of the temple. Then the Lord called to the man clothed in linen who had the writing kit at his side and said to him, "Go throughout the city of Jerusalem and put a mark on the foreheads of those who grieve and lament over all the detestable things that are done in it" (Ezekiel 9:1-4).

Here is a city that has almost totally apostatized, that has rebelled against God. That is why His great judgment has come upon it. That is why the people have been taken into captivity, and now God's judgment will fall upon those who still remain in the city. For as we look at this city through Ezekiel's eyes, we find them worshiping the stars of Heaven, erecting idols in the temple, and involving themselves in all kinds of abomination. They are corrupting and defiling the very house of God, and yet there is still this remnant who grieve over it, who weep because of it, who are hurt by all the corruption that is going on in the City of God. When God comes down in judgment, He sends one of His angels out and says, "Put a mark on the forehead of everybody who is grieved at what is happening here." Now the only people who are grieved when unrighteousness runs unchecked are those who are righteous. So it is the righteous who are being marked, and when God's judgment falls on the city, it is the righteous who will be preserved. So there is a mark on God's people that distinguishes them from every other inhabitant in the city. There is a mark on a remnant that shows that they belong exclusively to God, that they have not sold themselves to idolatry, that they have not given themselves to adultery. Here is a preserved, righteous remnant, and God says, "They will be Mine," and He puts His mark on them. Just as His mark on Cain preserved his life, so this mark on the people of Jerusalem preserved them from the judgment about to fall. The Book of Revelation is a book of God's judgments moving through the world, but God puts a mark on those who are His own.

A Mark of Separation

In Exodus God instructs Moses about the making of the garments for the High Priest:

> *Make a plate of pure gold and engrave on it as on a seal: Holy to the Lord. Fasten a blue cord to it to attach it to the turban; it is to be on the front of the turban. It will be on Aaron's forehead, and he will bear the guilt involved in the sacred gifts the Israelites consecrate, whatever their gifts*

may be. It will be on Aaron's forehead continually so that they will be acceptable to the Lord (Exodus 28:36-38).

The High Priest Aaron, when he went into the presence of God to minister, had a seal on his forehead. He wore a gold plate that distinguished him from everybody else; and on this gold plate this seal was engraved: "Holy to the Lord." What distinguishes God's people from every other people is that God's people are holy to the Lord. God's people recognize that they belong to Him. God's people understand that the world has no power over them, no influence upon them. You are not your own, you are bought with a price. On your forehead is written in indelible letters, sealed as on a gold crown, "Holy to the Lord." We are those who are preserved because of our righteousness. We are those who bear the holiness of God as a testimony upon our foreheads.

A Seal of Approval

When Jesus came into the world, He bore the seal of God. Talking about Himself as the Son of God, He says, "On Him God the Father has placed His seal of approval" (John 6:27). Jesus is sealed. He has a seal of approval on His life. The Church is sealed. Listen to what Paul says: "Nevertheless, God's solid foundation stands firm, sealed with this inscription: 'The Lord knows those who are His,' and, 'Everyone who confesses the name of the Lord must turn away from wickedness'" (2 Tim. 2:19). You have a seal, and it is a seal of ownership, for the Lord knows who are His. You have a seal, and it is a seal of approval because we turn away from wickedness.

A Seal of Holiness

So the seal of God that comes upon us is a demonstration of the life we live. We are not like everybody else. The church needs to wake up and realize that it is supposed to be different from the world. The first way it demonstrates its difference is by living differently. This does not mean going to meetings, carrying Bibles, or being miserable. The church is different from the world by its lifestyle, and its lifestyle is a lifestyle of holiness. We need to rediscover what it means to be holy. It is not in the old concept of holiness, whereby the holier you are, the more miserable you become; the holier you are, the bigger your Bible gets; the holier you are, the darker the suit you wear. That has got nothing to do with it. In fact, holiness and happiness are two sides of the same coin, because Psalm 45 says, "You love righteousness and hate wickedness; therefore God, your God, has set you above your companions by anointing you with the oil of joy." The holier you are, the happier you are supposed to be. That is how it works. There is a seal on us that distinguishes us, and it is a seal of holiness.

But of course, you and I both know that we cannot create a real sense of spiritual holiness in our own lives. If we try to do that, we are like Israel when they set out to establish their own righteousness. They just became legalistic. And sometimes our concept of righteousness is a list of dos and don'ts: "Do not handle! Do not taste! Do not touch!" (Col. 2:21). Those are the kind of things that often Christians try to adopt to present themselves as holy. It has nothing to do with that. The Kingdom of God is not eating and drinking, but righteousness, peace, and joy in the Holy Spirit. Now, we cannot create those things. We can create lists, we can create rules, and we can create regulations—and these were very much the essence of Old Covenant religion. But God has called us to something much different. God has called us to something much more glorious, and the holiness that we enjoy is not something that we create;

it is something that God imparts. Of course, it affects the way we live, but it is imparted to us, and so it motivates us.

The Seal of the Spirit

Let me take you to some New Testament Scriptures now.

Now it is God who makes both us and you stand firm in Christ. He anointed us, set His seal of ownership on us, and put His Spirit in our hearts as a deposit, guaranteeing what is to come (2 Corinthians 1:21-22).

Paul says every true believer has a seal. What is it? It is the Holy Spirit. What distinguishes you from everybody else on the face of the earth is this: God has anointed you and sealed you with His Spirit. What is the mark on the true church of Jesus Christ? What is the mark on the true believer? The Holy Spirit. Not the Holy Spirit who dwells in you in some theological way, not the Holy Spirit to whom you give some theoretical acknowledgment, but a demonstration. The seal is to be seen. The seal is to be read and recognized, and what God wants in your life and mine is a life so dominated by the Holy Spirit that He is the sole characteristic that we demonstrate to people. Here is a man full of the Holy Ghost. Here is a man upon whom the Spirit is resting. Here are the Lord's anointed ones. That is what the Church is supposed to be. That is what we as individuals are called to be, men and women marked out as different because of the anointing that is on us, the powerful, demonstrative anointing of the Holy Spirit. It is only the anointing of the Holy Spirit that will make you holy with the true holiness of Heaven; not in human holiness, but in divine holiness. Because He is the *Holy* Spirit, He will make you holy. What makes God's people different from every other people? It is the Holy Ghost, the Holy Spirit, somehow demonstrated through your life.

God said to John the Baptist that the Anointed One was coming. John asked how he was going to recognize him. God replies that it was the one upon whom he saw the Spirit descending and remaining (John 1:33). We are to be a people who were not just once baptized in the Spirit, but upon whom the Spirit remains, upon whom the Spirit rests, upon whom the anointing continually flows. We have been sealed. It is His mark of ownership on us. That is how you demonstrate, how you display, how you understand that you belong to God. You are full of the Spirit. You are moving in the Spirit. You are sensitive to the Spirit. You are at home when the Holy Ghost breaks out on every hand. It does not faze you. It does not frighten you. You are at home. And here is the wonderful thing. In all the manifestations, in all the dynamic diversities of the Spirit who moves among us, do you know it is only a deposit of what is yet to come? That is all it is. That which thrills you, which moves you, which stirs your heart and excites your spirit, is just the down payment. There is so much more to come!

In his letter to the Ephesians, Paul writes:

> *And you also were included in Christ when you heard the word of truth, the gospel of your salvation. Having believed, you were marked in Him with a seal, the promised Holy Spirit* (Ephesians 1:13).

You did not only get saved, you were included in Christ. That is wonderful. If any man is in Christ, he is a new creation. You were included in Christ but not just included in Christ; you were marked and sealed by the Holy Spirit. This is not just theology or theory. It is demonstrable relationship. The Holy Spirit comes, and it is evident that He has come. The Holy Spirit comes, and it is observable that He comes. The Holy Spirit comes and abides, and you live from this moment on in the power of the Holy Spirit. You live under the anointing of God. You live in signs and wonders and gifts of the Holy Spirit. You live from this moment on speaking in tongues and prophesying because it is the mark of God that is on you. We are called to be God's Holy Ghost people. There is no alternative. It is the only way. It is what God wants for us.

Paul also writes to the Ephesians, "And do not grieve the Holy Spirit of God, with whom you were sealed for the day of redemption" (Eph. 4:30). He is there, and so many have grieved Him, and as they have grieved Him, He has departed. So many have upset the Holy Ghost and in upsetting Him have lost the sense of His presence. We need to be those who do not grieve the Holy Spirit. We need to be those who do not despise prophecies. We need to be those who are open for all the manifestations of God because that is the effective mark of God that is on His people. We do not have to picture someone with a rubber stamp marking you on the forehead. This is the sign that you are a true child of God— you are full of the Holy Ghost. This is the sign that you are a true child of the King—you have been sealed with His Spirit. The anointing has come upon you and remains with you.

We are the people of God. This is not a sign for God's Pentecostal people. This is not a sign for God's charismatic people. This is a sign for all God's people. This is not a denominational thing. It is an ownership thing. You see, it is the Spirit and only the Spirit who makes Jesus real to you. You cannot even say Jesus is Lord except by the Holy Spirit. It is the Holy Spirit who takes the things of Christ and reveals them to you. He is the great teacher. You have an anointing that abides and teaches you all things (1 John 2:27). You cannot live, you cannot exist, and you cannot make any progress outside of the Holy Spirit. You must seek Him earnestly. You must obey Him completely. You must follow Him sensitively. We must rediscover in everything we do that we must be God's Holy Spirit people.

Overcoming by the Spirit

Now we are going to discover in the Scriptures that the Book of Revelation is not only encouraging us to be overcomers, but it is also teaching us *how* to be overcomers. We overcome because the Spirit of God is with us and the Spirit of God empowers us and the Spirit of God leads us.

A lot of the images that come into the Book of Revelation come from the prophet Zechariah. We have already looked there at the picture of the horses that he first presents in the opening chapters of his book. One of the great pictures and images, which we will discover later on is repeated in the Book of Revelation, is of those two olive trees in chapter 4. Do you remember the great picture of the two olive trees and the seven-branched lampstand and the oil that flows into them? He said the angel woke him up and he was like a man wakened from sleep. He is getting a night full of visions, so you can understand he is a bit weary, and the angel comes and wakes him up. He wakes him up in the middle of the night and asks what he sees. If he had done that to me, I'd probably have said, "Not much, actually. Nothing. Let me get a couple of cups of coffee and then ask me again." But he asks what he sees. He replies that he sees two olive trees and a lampstand. Then he asks the angel what it means. I like that about this prophet. Some people think prophets have all the answers. They actually don't, but they do know how to ask the right questions. He asks what it means. It's a very complicated vision. It's about olive trees and pipes and bowls and a lampstand. Actually the interpretation is quite simple. The angel says, "This is the word of the Lord to Zerubbabel: Not by might, nor by power, but by My Spirit, says the Lord of hosts" (Zech. 4:6). The whole of this complicated vision is interpreted with a simple statement. It is "by My Spirit, says the Lord." How are we going to overcome? "By My Spirit," says the Lord.

One of the things we are going to discover in the Book of Revelation is that there is a lot of mountain-moving going on. The Bible describes it in dramatic ways like, "the mountains flew away," and there are the disaster merchants who are looking for continents to disappear and nations to sink into the ocean and all kinds of stuff to be literally fulfilled. But that is just a dramatic way that God uses to show the removal of everything that opposes Him. When God speaks to Zechariah He says that it is not by might, nor by power, but by His Spirit, and then He continues by saying, "What are you, O mighty mountain? Before Zerubbabel you will become level ground" (Zech. 4:7). You see, it is when the anointing comes that the mountains fall. The Holy Spirit comes upon you and equips and empowers you to be God's people in a hostile world, not so that you can survive but so that you can overcome. Not just that you overcome, but that you actually invade the enemy territory. You tackle the mountain. You speak to it. Faith that moves mountains comes by the anointing of the Holy Spirit. Paul tells us it is one of the spiritual gifts that God operates in His Church. It is the anointing that is on you that marks you as the man or woman of God. It is the guarantee that you belong to the Lord.

Overcoming by the Word

There is another little insight here, too, that is important and interesting. When the beast, in his knee-jerk reaction to the Lamb, decides it is a good idea to have names written on things, he makes those who are under his control have a mark on their forehead or on their right hand. In some senses, that is a blasphemous travesty of what God required of His people, concerning His Word. For God told His redeemed people that they were to live by His Word, that His Word was not just a dusty moral code; it was a book to live by. If they walked in His ways, He would bless them. If they walked in His ways, He would keep them safe and they were to remind each other constantly of the Word. He said to talk about it together when you get up in the morning, when you go through the door, when you walk down the street, when you come home and lie down. Talk about the Word. Encourage each other in the Word. "Be so full of My Word," He says, "that you wear it as a phylactery on your forehead and on your hand because My Word will determine all of your thoughts and all of your actions. Have My Word on your forehead, have My Word on your hand, because I want you to be motivated in every situation in life by My Word." Of course, they turned that into an outward and legalistic thing, as they always did, but God wanted it to be a symbol of something that was going on in the inside.

Do you remember what He said to Joshua when Joshua was ready to take the people into the land of promise, when the Old Testament Jesus was about to bring the people out of the law?

Moses my servant is dead. Now then, you and all these people, get ready to cross the Jordan River into the land I am about to give to them. . . . Do not let this Book of the Law depart from your mouth; meditate on it day and night, so

that you may be careful to do everything written in it. Then
you will be prosperous and successful (Joshua 1:2,8).

God says, "My Word is to dominate your thinking. My Word is to be the declaration of your mouth. My Word is to be the demonstration of your life." We are to live by the Word of God. That is why, when Jesus came to Earth, He was the Word made flesh who dwelt among us. God's Word is not just to be on your head and on your hand, God's Word was designed to be in your heart. "I have hidden your word in my heart that I might not sin against you" said the Psalmist (Ps. 119:11). John writes, "I write to you, fathers, because you have known Him who is from the beginning. I write to you, young men, because you are strong, and the word of God lives in you, and you have overcome the evil one" (1 John 2:14). We overcome him because the Word of God is in us. It is the Word of God that motivates us. It is the Word of God that gives us the ability and the strength and equips us for all that God has called us to do. So we are people whose minds are dominated by the Word of God and whose actions are motivated by the Word of God. We must fill ourselves with the Word of God that we might speak it. From out of the fullness of the heart the mouth speaks. We are to be a people of the Word.

Now satan brings an evil counterfeit and puts a mark on their foreheads and their hands so that he and his evil ways dominate their thoughts. We are not like that. That mark has no effect upon us. We do not have to live with fear that somehow we have been enticed to take on the mark of the beast. It is not your credit card. It is not the bar code on the book that you buy or whatever you come to purchase in the supermarket. It is nothing that is outward in that sense. It has to do with the inner life. The mark of God is upon you. There is no room for the mark of the beast. The evil one has nowhere to place his mark. The mark of God on me is the anointing of the Holy Spirit who makes me holy. The mark of God on me is the name of Jesus that makes me live like Jesus lived. The mark of God on me is the inspiration of His Word that dominates my thoughts and determines my actions. This is how we know that we belong to God: we are full of the Spirit. This is how we know we belong to God: the anointing abides. This is how we know we belong to God: we perform the works that God sent us to do. The gifts of the Holy Spirit mark us as God's true sealed and delivered people, those who will not be touched by the power of the beast in his seduction to lead us away from the Lamb. He may put a mark on those who are his. He may, through them, pursue all kinds of persecutions against us, but we are sealed.

Before all the fury of judgment is released, God arises and sends forth His angel to seal you and to seal me, to say, "This one is mine; that one is mine. He belongs to me. She is My treasured possession, and this is how I will mark them: not by sticking a label on their inside, but by putting a flame of fire above their heads, by writing My name in big indelible letters across their foreheads. Sealed. Guaranteed. The deposit has been paid." There is more to come, more to see, more to experience, but this down payment is enough to keep you going through all the onslaught of the evil one, through all the opposition of the world, through all the cruelty of a fallen creation. You can stand tall. You can demonstrate the power of God because the Spirit of God is upon you. The Spirit of the Lord is upon me, for He has anointed me to preach good news to the poor, the opening of prison doors, the recovery of sight to the blind. We are marked with the Spirit of God! How do we know we belong to God?

Because no one can do the works you do unless the Father is with him; and "I tell you the truth," says Jesus, "anyone who has faith in me will do what I have been doing. He will do even greater things than these, because I am going to the Father" (John 14:12), and "I am going to send the Holy Spirit, and He will mark you as My people and as My victorious ones in a hostile world." (Author's paraphrase).

CHAPTER 7

The Church and the Spirit

We have seen that the 144,000 is the total of the redeemed community. It is 12 multiplied by 12, multiplied by 1,000. This conveys to us the completeness of God's community. These are God's warriors, the Church militant. They are the Church on Earth with this one desire, to honor the King and bring in His Kingdom. It tells us in chapter 14 that they follow the Lamb wherever He goes, and the thing that distinguishes them as the people of God is that they are marked with a seal—they are full of the Holy Spirit. The Holy Spirit is that person of the Trinity who now abides among the redeemed people of God. He is here. He is among us.

The Sevenfold Spirit

When John writes the Revelation, he begins the first chapter, "John, to the seven churches in the province of Asia: Grace and peace to you from Him who is, and who was, and who is to come, and from the seven Spirits before His throne" (Rev. 1:4). He brings greetings to the Church from the Father, Son, and Holy Spirit, but he represents the Spirit as the seven spirits that are before the throne. I am sure that you realize and appreciate that there are not seven Holy Spirits. I am sure you understand that when John speaks of the seven spirits, he is meaning the fullness of the Holy Spirit. We have seen already that the number seven continually and repetitively, through the Book of Revelation, means the fullness, the plenitude of whatever is being spoken about; and so when he speaks about the seven spirits, he is speaking about the fullness of the Holy Spirit. Later he tells us that, before the throne, seven lamps were blazing. These are, he says, the seven spirits of God (Rev. 4:5). This fullness of the Spirit is actually represented to us way back in the Old Testament in Isaiah, where the prophet is describing the coming of the Son of David, the one whom God will give to be Savior and Redeemer. Isaiah describes Him like this: "The Spirit of the Lord will rest on Him—the Spirit of wisdom and of understanding, the Spirit of counsel and of power, the Spirit of knowledge and of the fear of the Lord" (Isa. 11:2). Note that there are seven characteristics listed. The Son of David is to be anointed with the sevenfold Spirit of God. He is anointed with the fullness of the Holy Spirit.

One of the great examples for us in the Old Testament is a strange man, full of enigma and mystery. His name is Samson, and the name means sun. Immediately we can relate him to Jesus, who is the Sun of Righteousness (Mal. 4:2). Samson, too, is a sun who shines. His life is described like this: "The Spirit of the Lord came upon him in power" (Judg. 14:6,19; 15:14). He is a very charismatic character. In fact, in some ways, he is like

Jesus because, in his death, he brought a greater delivery to the people of God than he ever did in his lifetime. Just as Jesus, through His death, destroyed the power of the devil, so Samson, in his death, pulled down a satanic empire as he destroyed their temple. It is also interesting to note that on the roof were people who came tumbling down to their death as Samson overcame that kingdom of darkness. And there were three thousand people in all who were destroyed in that one act, just as centuries later three thousand people are swept into the Kingdom by the preaching of the good news of the Gospel, under the anointing of the Holy Spirit.

Samson represents many things to us. One of the great things about Samson is this. Nobody could understand where he got his strength. That means he probably didn't look like Arnold Schwarzenegger because, if he did, then everyone would have known why he was so strong. But it was a mystery. They were mystified by his strength. He was probably just a regular-looking guy, and they could not understand why one so ordinary looking should exercise such strength. It was because his strength did not come through his physique; it came through his anointing. You will remember how he is foolish and plays around with the truth until he finally gives away that the power of his anointing is in his hair. But here is an interesting thing about Samson. When he hears that the Philistines are upon him and his head has been shaved, he says he will shake himself as at former times. He was a man who, when the Spirit was on him, shook himself. Now he actually had his long hair braided into seven locks so that, when he shook himself, seven locks of hair flew from the top of his head. It looked like flames of fire, seven of them, sitting on his head, demonstrating the anointing of the sevenfold Spirit that was on him in power and that enabled him to work the miracles of God. It is the fullness of the Spirit, His totality, that comes upon the people of God.

When we meet the Lamb of God in the Book of Revelation, we might think that the name "Lamb of God" portrays Jesus as cuddly, but when you actually read the description, it is rather scary. It says this:

> *Then I saw a Lamb, looking as if it had been slain, standing in the center of the throne, encircled by the four living creatures and the elders. He had seven horns and seven eyes, which are the seven spirits of God sent out into all the earth* (Revelation 5:6).

Certainly a disturbing image, if it is taken literally. But symbolically we are being told that Jesus has the fullness of the Spirit. He is all-powerful and all-perceiving. He had seven horns and seven eyes, which are the seven spirits of God sent out into all the earth. Jesus is the ultimate anointed one.

Seven Horns

He has seven horns. Horns in Scripture always represent power, or strength. "[God] will give strength to His king and exalt the horn of His anointed" (1 Sam. 2:10). This means that God will make the king strong. David was anointed with oil from a horn because the horn represents strength, and it is strength that comes by the anointing. From that day on, the Spirit of God came upon him. He was strong in the Lord and in the power of His might. Jesus has total strength. Jesus is ultimately vigorous. He has seven horns.

It is fascinating to recall that when God has brought His people out of the wilderness, when they have actually taken their first steps into the land of promise, when they are going to defeat all the nations of Canaan, to bring in the Kingdom of God, to inhabit a land flowing with milk and honey, they still have to fight for it! Although God had promised that He would give to them every place where the souls of their feet trod, that did not mean it was going to be a walkover. They had to fight. They had to overcome. The first obstacle that they had to overcome was the huge and heavily fortified city of Jericho. God had a very strange strategy, not one that would have come from Joshua's ingenuity. It was a divine strategy, and it was this: the walls of Jericho would fall flat when the priests blew seven horns. No Jericho, no city, no kingdom, no empire, no power of darkness can stand before Jesus, who has seven horns that bring all opposition crashing down. He is anointed with power.

Seven Eyes

Not only does Jesus have Holy Ghost vigor; He has Holy Ghost vision. He has seven eyes. That really is bizarre. Six eyes we could cope with, three each side, but where does the seventh one go? He has seven eyes, but not literally, of course. This is a symbol. It is a picture. It is conveying something to us. He has seven eyes because He is the all-seeing one. In fact, the concept of seven eyes comes to us from the Book of Zechariah:

> *"See, the stone I have set in front of Joshua! There are seven eyes on that one stone, and I will engrave an inscription on it," says the Lord Almighty, "and I will remove the sin of this land in a single day* (Zechariah 3:9).

> *"Who despises the day of small things? Men will rejoice when they see the plumb line in the hand of Zerubbabel.*

*(These seven are the eyes of the Lord, which range through-
out the earth.)"* (Zechariah 4:10).

The Jesus whom we serve sees everything. There is nothing
going on in our world, nothing happening in our universe, nothing occurring in the darkest recesses of the whole of creation that
He is unaware of. It is one of the constant and repetitive certain-
ties of Scripture that God is the all-seeing God. The Psalms tell
us that "from heaven the Lord looks down and sees all mankind"
(Ps. 33:13), that "He rules forever by His power, His eyes watch
the nations—let not the rebellious rise up against Him" (Ps. 66:7),
and that "the eyes of the Lord are on those who fear Him, on
those whose hope is in His unfailing love" (Ps. 33:18). This is good
news. When you think you are alone, when you think you are isolated, when you think you are lost and abandoned, when you
think nobody knows the condition you are in or nobody cares
about the pain you are bearing, His eyes are on you. The eyes of
the Lord are everywhere.

On one occasion in the history of the kings of the Old
Testament, a prophet rebuked a king who had once walked
faithfully with God, but now had compromised. Not confident in
the ability of God to help him in his latest crisis, he compromises
with the enemy. A prophet confronts him and the prophet says
this to him, "For the eyes of the Lord range throughout the earth
to strengthen those whose hearts are fully committed to Him" (2
Chron. 16:9). I like that. The idea that God sees everything could
be intimidating and, in fact, if you are being sinful, should be
intimidating. You can do it in a corner, but God sees. You can do it
in the darkened room, but God sees. And yet God does not tell us
that He has the all-seeing eyes, that He has eyes that roam
throughout the earth, to scare us. God tells us that to encourage

us. The eyes of the Lord range throughout the earth to strengthen the hearts of those who are fully committed to Him. When you think you are lost and abandoned, He sees, and He sees not just as an idle observer, He sees not through the microscope of some bizarre heavenly experiment. He looks down and is moved with compassion for you. He sees, and having seen, He comes to deliver.

The writer to the Hebrews tells us this: "Nothing in all creation is hidden from God's sight. Everything is uncovered and laid bare before the eyes of Him to whom we must give account" (Heb. 4:13). When we see Jesus, we see Jesus as the ultimate Christ. We see Jesus as the absolute anointed one. He has seven horns and seven eyes. He has all power, and He sees all things. He sees where you are, and He is not fazed by your problems. His eyes examine. His eyes see all the repercussions. His eyes see all the elements. His eyes see your situation more fully and more clearly than you see it yourself. But the difference between Him and you is that He has power to resolve it. He has all power to change it because He is the anointed one, because He has the Spirit without measure. He has the fullness of the Holy Spirit.

Seven Lamps

In chapter 1 we noticed that the churches were represented by seven golden lampstands. Now, here is a great revelation and deep insight: a lampstand is designed specifically and expressly to have a lamp stood on it. In fact, it has no other function at all. It has no purpose other than to have a lamp on it. So down in Asia we see seven churches, and those seven churches are represented by seven lampstands. In chapter 4, John goes up into Heaven and, before the throne, he sees seven lamps blazing. Can we make the connection? Down here on Earth, seven lampstands. Up there before the throne, seven blazing lamps. Now, this isn't exactly a Mensa challenge, but do you think perhaps that there may be some kind of connection between seven lampstands and seven blazing lamps? It isn't rocket science. You see, the church was designed to be the place where the Spirit abides, because just as Jesus is the ultimate anointed one, it is this Jesus who presents Himself among the lampstands. To one of the churches He introduces Himself as He who holds the seven Spirits of God and His word to them is this: "Wake up!" because He wants to come with revival. He wants to bring the Spirit to them. They have a reputation that they are alive, but they are dead. Reputation is a terrible thing. We do not want reputations. We want the Holy Ghost. We might get a bad reputation if we get a lot of the Holy Ghost. We can cope with that. But you see, Jesus is not satisfied with the lampstand if it does not have a lamp on it.

There are churches around the world, and all they do on a Sunday morning is polish the lampstand. They stand back and admire the lampstand. They talk about the history of the lampstand. They look at the lampstand from different angles. But if there is no lamp on the lampstand, then it has not function! In fact, all you can do with it is murder Reverend Green in the library. The lampstand was designed to take the lamp. The church is designed to be full of the Holy Ghost. That is what it is for. You see, sometimes the truth of God has been hijacked. What God determined to be a demonstration of the Spirit has been turned into an intellectual exercise.

When Jesus came and taught that great Sermon on the Mount, He said to His disciples,

"You are the light of the world. A city on a hill cannot be hidden. Neither do people light a lamp and put it under a

bowl. Instead they put it on its stand, and it gives light to everyone in the house. In the same way, let your light shine before men, that they may see your good deeds and praise your Father in heaven" (Matthew 5:14-16).

In the Bible, good works are clearly defined for us when Peter speaks to Cornelius. He said: "God anointed Jesus of Nazareth with the Holy Spirit and power, and.... He went around doing good and healing all who were under the power of the devil, because God was with Him" (Acts 10:38). This kind of good works is not selling flags on Memorial Day. That may be a good work, but that is not the good works that the Scripture is talking about. The good works that Jesus did were works of power. The good works that Jesus did were Holy Spirit works. The good works that Jesus did delivered people from the power of satan, healed the sick, cleansed the leper, and raised people from the dead. Those were the good works, and our good works are supposed to create repentance and faith in the sight of those who see what is going on.

It is true that God's Word is also a lamp and a light: "Your word is a lamp to my feet and a light for my path" (Ps. 119:105). John the Baptist was described by Jesus as a lamp that burned and shone. The writer of the Proverbs tells his son that the instruction and the commandment is a lamp (Prov. 6:23), and so actually Scripture brings together two concepts: Word and Spirit. In actual fact, they are not two concepts. We sometimes hear people speaking like this: "He is a Holy Spirit man," or "He is a Word man." But if you are a Word man, the Word will take you to the Holy Spirit. If you are a Holy Spirit man, the Spirit will take you to the Word, because He is the author of the Word and He is the instigator of every demonstration.

The Church is to be the place where the Word is declared in clarity and where signs and wonders are performed in power. The church is the place where the Spirit comes and makes Himself known. The seven spirits that blaze before the throne of God want to come down and settle on the seven lampstands that are the Church. The Church without the Spirit is not a church. The Holy Spirit is looking for somewhere to feel at home. He came out of the sky in a bodily form like a dove and He rested Himself on Jesus. Now the Church is Christ in the world since Jesus went back to the Father, and the Spirit is looking, like the dove out of the Ark, for somewhere to set down His feet, looking for somewhere to rest and abide in order to manifest His power.

If we are going to be God's overcoming people, if we are to be God's triumphant and conquering people, if we are to be the people who bring the Kingdom into this hostile world—and that is what we are called to do—it will not be by might, nor by power, but by the Spirit, and the Spirit will always demonstrate Himself by acts of power.

Before the Throne

These seven spirits are said to be before the throne. This is the place where men stand in readiness to serve the Lord. The Spirit is the great servant of God. That does not diminish Him in any way. He comes to serve the purposes of God, and He stands before the throne of God in order to fulfill the purposes of God. Let me picture it this way. Here is the throne, and the Father sits upon the throne; and here are seven lamps blazing before the throne, and there is a sense of something not right. There is a sense of something missing, for the Son had gone down into the world to redeem lost humanity. He has paid the price for our sin. The Lamb had been slain, and on the third day He rose again. His work on the earth has been completed. He has been down into the bowels of hades and preached the good news to those who were waiting in anticipation of their own redemption. He has led the vanquished hosts out of their captivity. He has led captivity captive, and the great procession of Jesus has swept up through the skies.

There He went at the front of the parade. Behind Him came Moses, Abraham, David, Elijah, and all the dead saints who had been looking for the city, all the dead saints who had seen His day and had known that they had been preaching and prophesying about Him, now here He was. Their day had arrived. They came out of the shadows. They came out of sheol, and they went up in His procession, and as He approached the great heavenly city, He called out to the gatekeepers, "Lift up your heads, O you gates; be lifted up, you ancient doors, that the King of glory may come in." And all the angels on the battlements said, "Who is this King of Glory?" He said, "The Lord mighty in battle. Lift up. I am coming in!" (Ps. 24:7-10), and He led captivity captive and took them into the presence of the Father. He came to the throne, sat down in the middle of the throne, took the seven blazing lamps and threw them down onto the earth. "Exalted to the right hand of God, He has received from the Father the promised Holy Spirit and has poured out what you now see and hear" (Acts 2:33).

There is a demonstration when the Spirit comes. There are things to see and things to hear when the Spirit moves. May God help us! Help us to recapture the dynamic of the Gospel. Help us to become those who do not rely on our own strategy, organizational abilities, or oratory skills. Let us be those who rely on the Holy Ghost. Let us be those who know what it is to be anointed. Let our churches be full of that sound of the mighty rushing wind, as happened on the day of Pentecost, that from out of us might flow the good news of the Gospel that will touch the ends of the earth. Fill us with your Spirit, O God. Let the water of life flow from the temple and bring life wherever it goes to our lost and hurting and hungry world. Let us take the lamp and set it on the lampstand. It is not just the word that we preach, but the works that we do that will give light to all who come into the house.

Isn't it good that everyone who comes into our house is going to be enlightened, that everyone who comes into our house is going to come out of darkness into His most marvelous light? Everyone is going to see the presence of God. Why? "But if an unbeliever or someone who does not understand comes in while everybody is prophesying, he will be convinced by all that he is a sinner and will be judged by all, and the secrets of his heart will be laid bare. So he will fall down and worship God, exclaiming, 'God is really among you!'" (1 Cor. 14:24-25). How are people going to know that God is with us? They will know when the Holy Ghost manifests Himself. That is how. When God turns up in all His power and manifests His glory. God requires churches like that because that is how He designed them to be. They are the places where the Spirit is. They are the places where the Spirit makes Himself known. They are the places where the Spirit demonstrates His power. That is the kind of Church that Jesus died for.

Now many people point out that the Church is an eternal thing and that the Church was in the Old Testament; I believe all that, but just let me speak in a poetic sense. The Church, on the day of Pentecost, was brought forth in Holy Ghost fire, for not only was there the sound of a mighty rushing wind, there appeared tongues of fire that sat upon them. Just as Samson would shake his head and these great locks stood up in seven wonderful braids, so upon those in the upper room seven tongues of fire sat on each one of them as they were filled with the fullness of the Holy Spirit. One hundred and twenty people (ten multiplied by twelve) impacted the world in one moment of time. It sounds like God's strategy for success to me.

I believe in every effort that is made to win the lost. By all means save some (1 Cor. 9:22). There are many devices that have come. There are many strategies that have been devised. There are many methods that are happening in our world right now. You have user-friendly services. You have all kinds of things going on. That is fine, but I have a sneaky feeling in my heart that God's strategy, God's way forward, God's will to reach the lost is by a powerful anointing, by demonstrations of the Holy Spirit, by signs and wonders. It seems to me as I read the Scriptures that is what He designed the Church to be. That is the way that it came into visible being. It came with every accompaniment of Holy Ghost demonstration: fire and wind. He will baptize you, said John, in the Holy Spirit and with fire. He comes with power to equip us to be His people.

When Jesus, risen and among His disciples, began to give them commandments through the Holy Spirit, it was a new day. He did not just give them commandments from Himself, because He occupied a new place now. He gave them commandments "through the Holy Spirit" (Acts 1:2). The Holy Spirit was now the agent of the Son to communicate His will to the people. He was speaking to them about the Kingdom, and in their lingering ignorance they asked if it was at this time He was going to restore the kingdom to Israel. Bad question. Jesus does not answer it, but He lifts it into a new dimension.

> *He said to them: "It is not for you to know the times or dates the Father has set by His own authority. But you will receive power when the Holy Spirit comes on you; and you will be my witnesses in Jerusalem, and in all Judea and Samaria, and to the ends of the earth"* (Acts 1:7-8).

Two points are made here. "Lord, will *You* restore the kingdom?" Jesus says, "*You* will receive power." How? "When the Holy Spirit comes upon you." It's as if He said, "You are going to go out into the world and preach the Gospel, but wait in Jerusalem until you are endued with power from on high." If this first-century Church is going to impact its hostile environment, if the Church of King Jesus is going to impact the empire of Caesar, it will not do it by cunning, or by craft; it will not do it by intellect, skill, or ability. It will do it by an anointing that is irresistible. It will do it by an anointing that is unanswerable, by an anointing that is unquenchable, by a blazing lamp that sits on a receptive lampstand: the church that knows that its only reason to live is because the Spirit has chosen to live among them.

O God, let every one of your churches, let every congregation of your people and every gathering of your saints, be marked by this one thing: demonstrations of the presence of your Spirit that will glorify Jesus.

CHAPTER 8

An Earth-Shaking Kingdom!

When we look into the Word of God, we discover that the purpose of God is to bring His Kingdom into our world. For example, Jesus told the disciples that when they pray, they should pray like this: "Our Father in Heaven, hallowed be Your name, Your Kingdom come, Your will be done on earth as it is in Heaven" (Matt. 6:9-10). In recent years, the church has woken up to the truth that it is not here waiting to be taken away to the Kingdom; it is here to be proactive in prayer and ministry to bring the Kingdom down to Earth. It is self-evident when we read the Scriptures. When God planted a garden, it was His initial manifestation of a Kingdom on Earth, where He ruled and fellowshiped with Adam. God planted a garden, and He had a river flow out of the garden into four headwaters, dramatically demonstrating that His heart and purpose was to turn the whole world into the garden of the Lord, that the river was to be exported to the four corners of the earth. The Book of Revelation tells us that this is what is happening in everything that we experience on Earth. Whether it is the blessings of God in power to anoint and equip us to declare His Kingdom, or whether it is the disciplines and judgments that fall on a rebellious world, everything is geared to bringing in His Kingdom. Everything that God does is to this end—that the Kingdom might come.

God's Righteous Judgment

Judgment is one of the ways that God's righteousness is demonstrated and by which His Kingdom comes. The prophet Isaiah said that when God's judgments come to the earth, the citizens of the world learn righteousness (Isa. 26:9). That is the plan and purpose of God.

Evangelical thinking sometimes equates words that actually do not mean the same thing. In evangelical thinking we often equate judgment with condemnation. If we talk about God judging, we see it as a negative thing. If we talk about God bringing His judgments into the world, we see it as some kind of destructive visitation. The Bible knows nothing of such a concept because God's judgments are always redemptive and creative. That is how they operate. To illustrate this, consider the book in the Bible called the Book of Judges. The Book of Judges helps us understand how God's judgment works. Here we find God's people in rebellion, in apostasy, following and pursuing false gods, worshiping idols, and then discovering that there are divine repercussions to their actions. They come under pressure from their godless neighbors. They become enslaved to other societies, and, in their desperation, they call out to God, and Judges tells us that, at such times, God would raise up judges who delivered them. Not judges who condemned, not judges who came and kicked them when they were down, but judges who delivered them. God's judgments are geared to produce deliverance.

When Paul is writing to the Corinthian church, he has to confront them with a very serious problem. There is an incestuous situation in the congregation. As if this were not terrible enough, instead of rectifying it, they were almost blasé about it, apathetic toward it, and accepting of it. Paul is outraged in his righteous spirit and he says, "I want you to know I have already judged that man." Christian thinking in these sentimental (rather than biblical) days often carries the concept that it is always wrong to judge. People will say, "I know his life is not right, I know the relationship is a little bit questionable, I know his attitude might not be good, but do not judge him." Why not? That is exactly what we are supposed to do! "Oh no, brother, do not judge or you will be judged." Jesus said that we should judge with a *right* judgment because with the judgment I used to judge, I too will be judged (Matt. 7:1-2). So if I judge righteously, I know I am going to be judged righteously. If the church does not learn to judge, it will never learn to rule.

It is with this very issue that Paul confronts the Corinthians as he reviews their terrible situation and confronts them not doing anything about it. He says, "I have decided to deliver such a one to satan for the destruction of his flesh" (1 Cor. 5:5 NASB). This is an extreme measure. He says, however, he is acting so that the transgressor's spirit may be saved. This extreme judgment is being given not to destroy the man, but to bring him to repentance and faith because God's judgments are always creative.

Now the interesting thing to note is that Paul's comments on this situation in Corinth become a trigger for him to move on and say to them: "By the way, you should not be taking each other to court; if you do that you have already lost; whoever wins, you have both lost. Is there not anyone competent in the church to make these kinds of judgments?"

And then comes this throwaway line. It is a remarkable line. He doesn't elaborate on it. He doesn't teach on it. He simply says, "Do you not know that the saints will judge the world?" (1 Cor. 6:2).

And we sit there thinking, "No! I didn't know that! Tell me more!"

"Do you not know that we will judge angels? How much more the things of this life!" (1 Cor. 6:3).

"No, tell me more!"

But he doesn't tell us any more. However, what he is telling us is this: this time on earth is a probation period to see what God will entrust us with in the age to come.

The church is here to administer the justice of God. When we read the Book of Revelation, we find God administering justice in our world, and often that justice is administered through His church. We read for example, how God sends out plagues upon our world and yet, in chapter 11, there are two witnesses who turn the water into blood, who shut the skies so that it will not rain, and call down all sorts of plagues. It is God's representatives on earth who are actually the implementers of His divine judgments. The church is here to be the executors of God's divine purpose. I want to show you some of the ways that John, in the Book of Revelation, highlights that to us.

The Thunder and the Throne

In chapter 4, John goes up into the throne room of Heaven. We have looked at chapters 4 and 5, but I just want to take one particular picture that he sees. He describes the throne of God to us:

> *From the throne came flashes of lightning, rumblings and peals of thunder. Before the throne, seven lamps were blazing. These are the seven spirits of God* (Revelation 4:5).

God's throne is a noisy place. God's throne rumbles and thunders. From God's throne come flashes of lightning. It is a remarkable storm picture of a God who is enthroned over all things. The qualities of the throne are important for us to take note of. Thunder, rumbling, and lightning accompany the throne of God. So when we read of thunder, of rumbling, and of lightning, it should immediately remind us that these are the very qualities of the throne of God that is established in the Heavens. It is not soft clouds and harp music; there is dramatic stuff going on up there. In the presence of God there are clashes of thunder and flashes of lightning and those rumbling aftershocks that touch you and move you when the great thunderclaps of God have filled the air. It is an awesome place. It is a remarkable place. And the interesting thing is that after the last seal is opened, the last trumpet blown, and the last bowl poured out, those same manifestations are seen on the earth. Let me show you this:

> *When he opened the seventh seal, there was silence in heaven for about half an hour. And I saw the seven angels who stand before God, and to them were given seven trumpets. Another angel, who had a golden censer, came and*

stood at the altar. He was given much incense to offer, with the prayers of all the saints, on the golden altar before the throne. The smoke of the incense, together with the prayers of the saints, went up before God from the angel's hand. Then the angel took the censer, filled it with fire from the altar, and hurled it on the earth; and there came peals of thunder, rumblings, flashes of lightning and an earthquake (Revelation 8:1-5).

Let us imagine the scene. Here is the throne of Heaven. It sounds like thunder and rumblings and it is filled with flashes of lightning. But it goes quiet when it is about to move location out of Heaven on to earth. We are seeing in action the answer to the prayer, "Your Kingdom come." The throne is descending out of the Heavens, down onto the earth, and when it hits the earth, it shakes it. That's why there is an earthquake.

One of the ways that the prophets describe God's impacting of our world is by an earthquake. We do not have to be earthquake watchers, ticking off how many there have been to see how close His coming is. That is not what this is about. These are pictures and symbols. Whenever God comes into our world, He shakes it. That is what He does. There is an earthquake. The earthquake is not in Heaven—then it would have to have been called a Heaven-quake! When it comes on earth, it shakes our world. So the climax of all the undoing of the seven seals is to bring God's Kingdom down on earth. That is God's whole purpose. That is why the book has been undone. It is to set in motion the purposes of God, whose climax is to have His Kingdom down here on the earth, so that the cry can go up, "The seventh angel sounded his trumpet, and there were loud voices in Heaven, which said: 'The kingdom of the world has become the

Kingdom of our Lord and of His Christ, and He will reign for ever and ever'" (Rev. 11:15). The Kingdom comes with violence. It shakes our world. In fact, the writer to the Hebrews describes it like this:

> *At that time His voice shook the earth, but now He has promised, "Once more I will shake not only the earth but also the heavens." The words "once more" indicate the removing of what can be shaken—that is, created things—so that what cannot be shaken may remain. Therefore, since we are receiving a Kingdom that cannot be shaken, let us be thankful, and so worship God acceptably with reverence and awe, for our "God is a consuming fire"* (Hebrews 12:26-29).

Then he tells us that we are receiving a Kingdom that cannot be shaken. God is going to shake all the kingdoms of this world. God is going to shake our planet, and that will be a demonstration of the coming of His Kingdom.

Again in chapters 11 and 16 of Revelation (11:15-19; 16:17-21) God intervenes dramatically with the affairs of our world. We read of His throne coming among the nations of this world to such a degree that we find, in the final rendering of this drama, that the great city, which is Babylon and represents everything that is evil, is split in three. The cities of the world collapse because everything that can be shaken has been shaken, and only the Kingdom of God is going to be established and permanent in our world. We are seeing God's throne coming down onto the earth, and it is the climax of all the judgments that God fulfills through the other seals, the other trumpets, and the other bowls of wrath. Each of them leads up to this great climax where God's rule is demonstrated in the world.

God's Hailstones

Now, of course, you know I am sure that all these things are symbolic. All these things are signs. This is not history written in advance. We do not have to be worried about thrones falling out of the sky. We do not have to be worried about huge hailstones, one hundred pounds each falling on us and terrifying us. What God is saying is, "Listen, I am going to shake this world. I am going to interfere with the plans and the schemes of men because I have determined that this world will be filled with My glory. I have determined that the kingdoms of this world will become the Kingdom of My power and of My Christ." You will notice that in the latter two incidents, of the seventh trumpet and the seventh bowl, the storm was accompanied by hailstones. Hailstones actually represent God at war. They are the weapons of His warfare. So it tells us that God is coming down as a warrior to establish His Kingdom. Listen to what God said to Job:

> *Have you entered the storehouses of the snow or seen the storehouses of the hail, which I reserve for times of trouble, for days of war and battle?* (Job 38:22-23)

God is a warrior and the weapon of His warfare is represented to us in Scripture as the hurling down of hailstones. One of the most dramatic moments when God did that is in Joshua chapter 10. Joshua is pushing forward, in obedience to the Word of God, to take the land of Canaan. The taking of Canaan by Israel, by the way, is a very important period. The books of Joshua and Judges are extremely relevant to us because they are a picture of Israel taking the land, and it is a forerunner of how the Church is to take the world. Joshua, the Old Testament Jesus, is leading the troops forward. He is pressing his advantage to overcome the enemy and bring in the kingdom, but he knows he is running out of time. He knows that he will not get this task fulfilled if darkness comes. He needs the light to remain with him, and in a stroke of incredible boldness he says, "O sun, stand still over Gibeon, O moon, over the Valley of Aijalon," and they stood still in the sky (Josh. 10:12)! God gave him a unique day in which to gain his victory, and as the enemy ran away from Joshua's pursuit, God hurled great hailstones down upon them. The Bible tells us that there were more killed by the hailstones that God hurled than by the swords of Joshua's troops.

God joined in the battle and routed the enemy, and He did it on a unique day. In fact, the Bible says there has never been a day before or since like that day. This is the day that Habakkuk wanted God to renew. Do you remember when we read Habakkuk, chapter 3, and he condenses all the great works of God into one wonderful psalm? He says, "O God, the sun stood still and the moon did not move. O Lord do it again in our day." There was a desire for a new kind of day. The closing chapter of the Old Testament promises a new kind of day. For God says, "But for you who revere my name, the sun of righteousness will rise with healing in its wings. And you will go out and leap like calves released from the stall" (Mal. 4:2). Two thousand years ago the sun of righteousness rose and never ever set again. We have been in a new day for two thousand years!

If you have been around a prophetic people for very long, you will find that there are certain expressions that occur again and again, whoever prophesies. I am not making fun of it; it just happens. One of the things we hear repeatedly is, "Thus says the Lord, it is a new day." Well, it has been a new day for two thousand years; it is just that some of us are just beginning to wake up to it. It is a new kind of day. It is a miracle day. Mary went down with the women to anoint Jesus' body while it was still dark. But He was up already because the Son rose before the sun rose—and ushered in God's new day. We might think it is nighttime, but that is only because we are asleep. That is why Paul says, "Wake up, O sleeper, rise from the dead, and Christ will shine on you" (Eph. 5:14). Why? Because He is up already! You wake up and say it is a new day, and Jesus says it has been like that for a long time. And in God's new day, He hurls down His weapons of warfare on those who would resist Him.

Hail is one of the plagues that God sent on Egypt. When God hurled down hailstones that killed men and cattle and flattened all the crops and stripped all the trees bare, the whole land of Egypt was devastated except for one place, and that is where the people of the Lord lived. The weapons of His warfare are directed toward the unrighteous. He wants to bring them to repentance. He wants to remove them from among His enemies. Listen to what Isaiah says:

> *Though hail flattens the forest and the city is leveled completely, how blessed you will be, sowing your seed by every stream, and letting your cattle and donkeys range free* (Isaiah 32:19-20).

While God's enemies are being devastated, God's people are being blessed. God is at war with His enemies, but we are at peace with God through Jesus. It would be a wise and sensible thing for the world to wake up and realize that to be God's enemy is to be a perpetual loser. To think for a moment, to imagine for the wildest second, that I could resist the living God is utter foolishness. The sensible thing is to give up and give in. But the history of the world tells us that it does not usually happen like that. Pharaoh experienced again and again the plagues of God, but all that happened was that his heart grew harder. And did you notice that when God devastates the city in chapter 16, that rather than bow the knee and confess His lordship, men cursed God? What a crazy world! But these dramas that are enacted here are pictures of the power of God and of the unstoppable nature of God in the face of the most severe opposition. Nothing can stand against our God. His throne will be established in the earth. His Kingdom will stretch over all the nations.

God's Mobile Throne

Ezekiel chapter 1 comes at a moment of great sadness for the people of God. They have been exiled. They have been carried away from their homes. They are in Babylon, and Ezekiel says, "In the thirtieth year." That is almost certainly Ezekiel's thirtieth year. He is thirty years of age. It is the age that he would have come into the fullness of the priestly ministry to which he was ordained. But now he has been taken into captivity. He may have had the great ambition that one day he would go behind the curtain on the Day of Atonement with the incense smoke to sanctify the people of God. That moment will now never come. The curtain will never be parted for him. He has been carried away into captivity, but although he may never see the curtain parted, Heaven is opened, just as it was to be for John on Patmos centuries later, and he sees God coming on His Heavenly chariot. He sees God coming on His mobile throne! He describes it like this:

> *In the thirtieth year, in the fourth month on the fifth day, while I was among the exiles by the Kebar River, the heavens were opened and I saw visions of God. On the fifth of the month—it was the fifth year of the exile of King Jehoiachin—the word of the Lord came to Ezekiel*

the priest, the son of Buzi, by the Kebar River in the land of the Babylonians. There the hand of the Lord was upon him. I looked, and I saw a windstorm coming out of the north—an immense cloud with flashing lightning and surrounded by brilliant light. The center of the fire looked like glowing metal, and in the fire was what looked like four living creatures. In appearance their form was that of a man (Ezekiel 1:1-5).

He sees this throne with all these Heavenly manifestations. God's throne is on the move, and, although God's people are in captivity, although God's people are in defeat, although a powerful enemy has overcome God's people, God's throne is not overcome, God's purpose is not thwarted, and God's plan has not been abandoned. His throne is still intact, and His throne manifests itself even in places where it looks as if His people have been overcome. The one who sits on the throne has not abdicated, and the great thing is this: you may not hear the thunder, you may not see the lightning, you may not experience the great cloud formations that surround the throne of God, but that is how God comes to you.

It would be exciting to experience it in the Spirit as David did. At least if he did not see it and experience it, God revealed what was happening in his inner man and illumined his spirit with the reality of His visitation. Psalm 18 is a song of thanksgiving that David gives to God for a personal deliverance. He is not talking about saving the nation or about bringing in the Kingdom; he is talking about God saving him. Listen how he expresses it:

The earth trembled and quaked, and the foundations of the mountains shook; they trembled because He was angry.

Smoke rose from His nostrils; consuming fire came from His mouth, burning coals blazed out of it. He parted the heavens and came down; dark clouds were under His feet. He mounted the cherubim and flew; He soared on the wings of the wind. He made darkness His covering, His canopy around Him—the dark rain clouds of the sky. Out of the brightness of His presence clouds advanced, with hailstones and bolts of lightning. The Lord thundered from heaven; the voice of the Most High resounded. He shot His arrows and scattered the enemies, great bolts of lightning and routed them. The valleys of the sea were exposed and the foundations of the earth laid bare at your rebuke, O Lord, at the blast of breath from your nostrils. He reached down from on high and took hold of me; He drew me out of deep waters (Psalm 18:7-16).

Do you know when God took hold of you that is how He came? You may not have heard it. You may not have seen it, but that is what happened. There are all kinds of enigmas in the manifestation of God's presence. He is clothed in darkness, but the brightness of His presence shines. How do you work that out? I do not know! Sometimes they describe it all, and sometimes they describe elements of it. Paul, or Saul as he was then, is on his murderous way on the Damascus Road, and he discovers the presence of God breaking into his life like a light that shines brighter than the sun. Although it happened at midday, the brightest moment of our natural sun, there was a light that broke on him that was brighter than the sun. God breaks into our lives like this. God seeks you like this.

He rescued me from my powerful enemy, from my foes, who were too strong for me. They confronted me in the day of my disaster, but the Lord was my support. He brought me out into a spacious place; He rescued me because He delighted in me (Psalm 18:17-19).

God is for you. When God comes to rescue you, He comes just like that! I guess in some ways it is a blessing that we do not see it—we might die of fright before we ever got rescued! But God brings His throne down into your circumstances and lifts you out of them. And just as God comes to you by manifesting His rule where you are, that is what He does in our world. God comes down into our world to manifest His rule. His ultimate purpose, of course, is that men and women would be saved. Whenever God comes down, these phenomena are recorded. It happened when He came down on Mount Sinai to make this rescued rabble into a holy nation, when He came down to communicate His Word to His people. Listen how it is described in Exodus chapter 19:

> *On the morning of the third day there was thunder and lightning, with a thick cloud over the mountain, and a very loud trumpet blast. Everyone in the camp trembled* (Exodus 19:16).

> *Mount Sinai was covered with smoke, because the Lord descended on it in fire. The smoke billowed up from it like smoke from a furnace, the whole mountain trembled violently* (Exodus 19:18).

There is an earthquake because God has come down. The sound of the trumpet grew louder and louder. God manifested Himself in the midst of His people as the one who rules in power. What an awesome visitation that was! How scared and awestruck the people were! It was a manifestation of unapproachable holiness. No one could come near the mountain; not even an animal could walk on the foothills of this mountain. If anyone did, they were to be killed. They could not come near the mountain; but we have a mountain on which God sits enthroned. And we are welcome, not only to come to the foothills of the mountain, but to ascend into the presence of the Lord, to know what it is like and to hear the sound of His throne. It is what happened to John in chapter 4 of Revelation. He went into the throne room and he saw what the throne was like so that he would recognize when the Kingdom came. He would hear the sound of the thunder and the rumblings and the lightning and he would think to himself, "I have been here before. That is what happened in Heaven. Now it is happening on earth."

What does it mean? It means the Kingdom is coming. It may come with judgments, it may come with pestilence, it may come with violence, but the Kingdom is coming. Whatever happens in our world is guaranteed by God to be one of the means of bringing in the Kingdom of Heaven. We should not be concerned. We should be concerned in a humanitarian way at the things that are happening in our world, but we should not be concerned in a fearful way. All these things are manifestations of the coming of God. Jesus told the people this: "You will hear of wars and rumors of wars, but see to it that you are not alarmed. Such things must happen, but the end is still to come" (Matt. 24:6). We used to be earthquake watchers, and the more earthquakes there were, the closer His coming. But Jesus said that the earthquake is a sign that the end is not yet come. What is the sign of the end? "The Gospel of the Kingdom will be preached in the whole world as a testimony to all nations, and then the end will come" (Matt. 24:14). Those rumblings, those earthly disasters, those famines and pestilences, those earthquakes that happen in the world, they are not the death rattles of a dying world but the birth pains of something new! They are the heralds of the Kingdom that is coming. They are the harbingers of a throne that will be established in our world.

In the song of Deborah and Barak, in the Book of Judges, they engage in what appears to be an isolated and localized fight, but actually it is something much more. They believe that what happened to them had cosmic significance, and they sing about it in these words:

> O Lord, when You went out from Seir, when You marched from the land of Edom, the earth shook, the heavens poured, the clouds poured down water. The mountains quaked before the Lord, the One of Sinai, before the Lord, the God of Israel (Judges 5:4-5).

They said, "When we went out to fight, God marched ahead of us. And when God marched ahead of us, when He put down His great holy legs on those sanctified feet, He shook the earth. When we went out to battle, the earth shook because God was with us." When you go out to battle, when you go out to win the lost, Jesus goes before you on His great legs of glory and shakes everything. Here is how David spoke about it, though here he is not going out to war but is bringing the Ark into Jerusalem. It is a time of worship and celebration, but David, never one to pass up a great line, takes hold of the words of Deborah and makes them his own:

> When you went out before your people, O God, when you marched through the wasteland, the earth shook, the heavens poured down rain, before God, the One of Sinai, before God, the God of Israel (Psalm 68:7-8).

When we go to worship, or when we go to war, we are affecting our world. When we go forward in the purposes of God, we go forward with an earthquake tremor. We go forward to shake the nations, to shake the cities, to see them crumble, to see them fall because our God goes before us on His great throne. He goes before us with thunder. He goes before us with rumblings. He goes before us with flashes of lightning, and everywhere His throne lands, there is an earthquake. There is a whole lot of shaking going on because God has come down into the midst of His people! His throne, established in Heaven, comes down and impacts our world and, by the heaviness of its glory, shakes our world, collapses opposition, and brings in the Kingdom. What happens in Revelation is happening in our world today.

CHAPTER 9

Voices from the Altar

We have already seen, in chapter 6 of Revelation, the Lamb unsealing the scroll, and we watched as he broke the first four seals and released the horsemen of God's purposes. But let us read on a little further:

> *When he opened the fifth seal, I saw under the altar the souls of those who had been slain because of the Word of God and the testimony they had maintained. They called out in a loud voice, "How long, Sovereign Lord, holy and true, until You judge the inhabitants of the earth and avenge our blood?" Then each of them was given a white robe, and they were told to wait a little longer, until the number of their fellow servants and brothers who were to be killed as they had been was completed (Revelation 6:9-11).*

As the Lamb breaks one of the seals, we actually see some of those who have preceded us into glory, the martyrs. One of the things about the Book of Revelation is that everyone is presented as a martyr. The word martyr literally means witness. An ultimate act of witness, of course, is laying down your life, but everyone in the Book of Revelation who is faithful to Jesus is considered to be a witness and therefore is numbered among the martyrs. Because we overcome the evil one, because we do not love our lives even so much as to shrink from death, we are counted among the martyrs. "Be faithful, even to the point of death, and I will give you the crown of life," says the Lord (Rev. 2:10). So even those who do not die are numbered among those who are willing to lay down their lives.

The Altar of Incense

We are therefore the witnesses of the Lord, and as Jesus breaks this fifth seal, we get a glimpse, under the altar, of the souls of those who have been martyred and slain because of their faithfulness to Jesus and the word of the testimony that they bore.

Most commentaries tell you that this altar is the bronze altar of sacrifice that is in the courtyard of the temple. I do not want to sound arrogant, but I do want to differ with what they say. I don't believe it is the bronze altar. If it is, it is the only place in the Book of Revelation that it is mentioned. But there are two pieces of temple furniture that are continually mentioned in the Book of Revelation. The throne, of course, is the Ark, because God is enthroned above the cherubim that cover the Ark of the Covenant. It is His mobile throne. It is the Ark where He sits in majesty and authority. The only other continually mentioned piece of furniture is the altar, described as "the altar that is before the throne." So the throne and the altar have a special relationship. The throne always represents the Ark, and the altar always represents the altar of incense. We will look at this in more detail later because it is a very important concept.

What is more, on two other occasions in the Book of Revelation we discover the altar of incense being vocal. A voice comes from the altar. It seems to me to be much more consistent to see those three times when the altar speaks as voices coming from the same altar. What is more, although these martyrs represent sacrifice because they have laid down their lives, this should not take us to the brazen altar, because that is the place where sacrifice was made to take away sin. My death will never take away sin. But there is another sacrifice of which Scripture speaks.

When God called Abraham to offer up his son Isaac, Abraham did it without hesitation. He did it without argument. He did it without any twinge of conscience because he had an unshakeable faith in the goodness of God. He had an unshakeable faith in the word of God's promise. God had promised him that through this son, through Isaac, all the families of the earth would be blessed. It was through Isaac, the son of the covenant, that God's promises would be fulfilled. So when Abraham went to Mount Moriah to offer up his son, he did not have a moral problem. He comes to the foot of the mountain and he says to the servants, "Stay here with the donkey while I and the boy go over there. We will worship and then we will come back to you" (Gen. 22:5). He really believes he is going to build an altar, and he does. He really believes he is going to lay the wood on the altar, and he does. He really believes he is going to bind his son and lay him on the altar, and he does. He really believes he is going to plunge in the knife, set fire to the wood, and offer up his son as a burnt offering, and he believes that out of the ashes, out of the remains of his child of promise, God will bring resurrection. And the writer to the Hebrews says that he received him back as a type (Heb. 11:19). The typology is remarkable, for just as Isaac carried the wood upon his shoulders, so Jesus went up to His mountain carrying on His shoulders the cross that was going to be the means of His sacrifice. Now God saved Abraham's son and showed him a ram as a substitute. But, in Abraham's understanding, this whole event was an act of worship. This is the first time that the word worship is used in Scripture for a prepared and deliberate act, and Abraham's offering of Isaac helps us to understand what true worship is. The incense altar was an altar of worship, and we see in the demonstration of Abraham's faith that worship is about sacrifice.

True worship is not singing songs, clapping, and raising hands in the presence of God. True worship is not shouting and jumping. It may include all those things, but true worship is laying down your life for God. So these martyrs, if you like, have entered into ultimate worship as they have yielded their lives to the Lord. Paul writes to the Romans like this:

> *Therefore, I urge you, brothers, in view of God's mercy, to offer your bodies as living sacrifices, holy and pleasing to God—this is your spiritual act of worship* (Romans 12:1).

Worship is giving myself utterly, totally, unconditionally to God. Therefore I am suggesting that those who are under the altar are those who have made the ultimate act of worship. They have given their lives for the Lord. And it has become pleasing and precious to Him. The psalmist believed this:

He will rescue them from oppression and violence, for precious is their blood in His sight (Psalm 72:14).

The blood of the righteous is precious to God. The life is in the blood, and therefore their lives are precious to Him. When we bring sacrifice to God, we do not bring things that are not worth anything. We do not bring things that are the dog-ends of what is left, of what we have enjoyed for ourselves and spent upon our own pleasures. We bring to God that which is precious. We bring to God that which is of value. We bring to God that which is costly, we give it to Him that He might take pleasure in it. The Bible tells us that "precious in the sight of the Lord is the death of His saints" (Ps. 116:15). There is preciousness about yielding your life to God.

The Fellowship of the Saints

So my conviction is that this altar, that we see here for the first time, is the altar of incense where ultimate sacrifice has been made by those willing to lay down their lives for Jesus. Now, the fascinating thing is that, having passed into His presence, they have not finished their ministry. When you and I go into the presence of the Lord, we do not go into some eternal slumber room. We do not go into some kind of beautifully proportioned and wonderfully furnished waiting room. We come into the presence of God, and we continue with ministry. I do not understand it all. The Bible is not clear about it all. There are those who have gone on before us, but, in some divine way in the eternal economies of God, they are still part of us. It is what the old Puritans used to call the fellowship of the saints. It is not that we speak to them. It is not that we pray to them. It is not that we invite them down to our séance. But there is a fellowship between us and those who have gone before us.

When we come together as the Church, when we gather as brothers and sisters, as co-workers, as friends together in the presence of Jesus, we ascend the mountain. It is a great revolution in our hearts when we understand that we are not here to invite Jesus to come to our meeting. Jesus invites us to come to His meeting. His meeting is up a hill. Every time we meet together we hear a voice that says, "Come up here." We ascend the hill of the Lord, and as we go up, we find ourselves coming into communion with the church of the firstborn, whose names are enrolled in Heaven.

We come to myriads and myriads, thousands and thousands and ten thousand times ten thousand angels who are gathered in festal assembly—that is, angels with their party clothes on. We come into the presence of God the Judge because the Church is the place where His judgments are pronounced. We come to Jesus, the mediator of a new covenant, and to the sprinkled blood that speaks a better word than the blood of Abel. But there is another group to which we come, in the same exercise of faith, as we enter the presence of God. That group is described as the spirits of righteous men made perfect (Heb. 12:22-24). There is a sense, without getting too mystical, that when we come together we fellowship with all the saints who have ever walked the path of faith because there is one eternal Church. The Church cannot be divided by denominations; the Church cannot be divided by nations, and the Church cannot be divided by dispensations. It is one Church from the beginning until the end. So there is a communion of saints that is real and yet a mystery.

After telling us that we have ascended the mountain, the writer of Hebrews tells us that in our earthly ministry we are to run the race that is set before us because we are surrounded by a cloud of witnesses. It would seem that not only do the spirits of righteous men find their rest in the Lord's Heavenly presence but they continue to be concerned for the purposes of God on earth. Observing the race of faith in which the Church is engaged, these righteous men eagerly await the final lap and the tape of ultimate victory. For this is when God's cosmic plan is finished and His Kingdom has come.

"How Long, O Lord?"

The concern of the Heavenly martyrs has caused some problems for modern Christians. It appears to be far too harsh and vengeful for current evangelical sensibilities. The Heavenly martyrs ask God in a loud voice, "How long, Sovereign Lord, holy and true, until You judge the inhabitants of the earth and avenge our blood?" (Rev. 6:10). Some people say that does not sound like a very Christian response. We should be more like Stephen, who, when he was being stoned, raises his eyes to Heaven, sees the Lord, and says, in effect, "God, don't judge them for this, don't hold it to their account" (see Acts 7:60). Shouldn't we be more like that? Well, as individuals, yes.

As individuals we turn the other cheek; as individuals we take the slander and the persecution of the world. As individuals who are persecuted for righteousness' sake we do not retaliate. But there is still an issue of justice, and the Church must be concerned not only with grace but also with justice. Those who have gone before us are concerned that God's justice be manifested in our world. We considered, in an earlier chapter, the throne coming down in judgment because it manifests the justice of God. Heaven is concerned that God's justice be manifested in the earth. Remember, these are pictures. They are symbols. It is not actually recording real events. We always have to remind ourselves of this so that we realize that we are not seeing something that actually happens; it is John communicating to us, as best he can by the inspiration of the Holy Spirit, attitudes and actions that are spiritual. What he is telling us here is that the saints who have gone before us are concerned with God's justice in the world. Although it is difficult for us to imagine and understand, there almost seems to be with them a sense of frustration. It almost seems as if they are losing patience.

"How long, O Lord?" is a familiar cry from the Scriptures. As you go through the Word of God, you will find again and again men, women, and nations crying to God, saying, "How long?" In fact, that should not surprise us because there are many of you reading this book now whose own hearts have cried at times and may be crying even today, "How long, O Lord? How long until You get me out of this problem? How long until You answer that prayer? How long until my loved one gets saved? How long until this disease is healed? How long until this prayer is answered?" There is a sense of longing in our hearts, almost a sense of desperation for God to do things that we have asked Him to do for a long, long time. We are not alone. It is all the way through the Scriptures. Listen to what the psalmist says:

> *My soul is in anguish. How long, O Lord, how long?* (Psalm 6:3)

> *How long, O Lord? Will You hide Yourself forever? How long will Your wrath burn like fire?* (Psalm 89:46)

He is under the discipline of God. He is under the hand of the Lord. Have you been here? If you have, you will know that it is a desperate prayer. But it is a biblical prayer. The church also has to learn to pray God's apparently delayed judgment on the wicked. How long? I am being persecuted. I am in anguish. I am not getting my prayers answered. How long, O Lord? How many of us can identify with Habakkuk:

> *How long, O Lord, must I call for help, but You do not listen?*
> (Habakkuk 1:2)

How long? This is a prophet of God. This is not the man who turns up occasionally to the cell group. This is a prophet of God. How long, O Lord, must I go on asking and You never answer? Here is an angel of the Lord speaking to God in Zechariah chapter 1:

> *Then the angel of the Lord said, "Lord Almighty, how long will You withhold mercy from Jerusalem and from the towns of Judah, which You have been angry with these seventy years?"* (Zechariah 1:12)

You thought you had waited a long time for the answer to your prayer. He has been waiting for seventy years. If we are honest, and I am sure we are, we will identify with that sense of frustration. We will identify with that sense of longing that says, "God, how long until we have breakthrough? How long until we have increase? How long until we have grace and growth? How long until we experience mercy and miracle?" It is a good prayer. It is a good prayer because it shows you mean business. It also helps us to understand that God's patience has greater endurance than ours. But there is this sense that pervades heaven and earth that is summed up with the cry, "How long?" We pray, "God, we want to see all Your purposes, all Your plans, Your power, and Your Kingdom; we want to see all of Your glory displayed and demonstrated in our lives, in our fellowships, in our cities, in our nations, in our world—and we want to see it now!"

So, how long? There are a number of answers to this fundamental question. The first and most important one is this: "Until." That is God's answer to these people: until the number of your fellow servants and brothers who are to be killed as you have been is completed. This helps us to understand God's timetable. For us time is a linear progression. Year follows year. It moves forward like a never-ending stream. God, of course, lives outside of time. Time came into being when God created the world. Until creation there was no time, there was just eternity.

Somebody once said that God created time just to stop everything from happening at once. But we live as captives of time; we live in a linear understanding of time. God has no such limitation. But because we are captives of linear time, it leads people to try to work out whereabouts down that line of time Jesus is going to come again. How many years is going to be? How many months? How many days? What feast is it going to correspond with? All this bizarre manipulation is to try to find the date on which He will come. Every date that has been predicted so far has not been fulfilled. I think that gives us confidence that the same will be true for every date they are going to predict in the future. God does not look at things in a linear way. They say "How long?" and God says, "Until the number has been fulfilled." It has got nothing to do with how many years are going to pass. It has got to do with how many people are going to die.

There is a big difference here. When God spoke to Abraham, entering into covenant with Him, He said, "Abraham, I am going to give you this land, but before that happens your people are going to go down into Egypt. They are going to be slaves, and then they are going to come back out after four hundred years." Now, God tells Abraham how many linear years it is going to take, but that is not how God judges it. God says they are going to come back in that number of years because the sin of the Amorites has not yet reached its full measure (Gen. 15:13-16). Because He is God, He knows that the full measure will be reached in three hundred years. He does not give this figure because that is the length of time He has determined, but because He knows that is how long it will take for the full measure to be reached. It is very important that we grasp this. We are not trying to work out dates. This is why Peter says that we not only look for the coming of Jesus but we can actually hasten it (2 Pet. 3:11-12). How? By living the kind of lives that God responds to, by seeking to get the Church to the place of fullness.

Jesus will come, not when the Church has been here a number of years, but when the Church comes to the fullness of the total measure of Christ (Eph. 4:13). That is why we can make a difference in our world. We are not slaves of cruel fate. We are the servants of a destiny planned by our loving Heavenly Father, and we can make a difference in our world. We can actually bring in the Kingdom and bring back the King.

The Blood that Speaks

God wants these martyrs first to be robed and clothed in white garments. Seven times we meet people in the Book of Revelation dressed in white, and every time it is a mark of their righteousness, of their holiness, of their sanctification. They are robed in white because they are God's pure people. They are told to wait a little while because they are God's patient people. We have need of patience in that after we have done the will of God, we will inherit the promises (Heb. 10:36). God also wants them to know that, without us, they will not be made complete because there are others yet to come, other martyrs who will lay down their lives, others to submit totally to Jesus. There is a divine interaction between Heaven and Earth. There is a communion between those who are militants still on the earth and those who have ascended into the presence of God. We are part of the same company. We are members of the same wonderful Church, and while here on earth we are praying at this altar. Meanwhile, those who have ascended into the presence are also crying to God for the fulfilling of His purposes. The idea, of course, of the dead speaking, praying, and calling on God comes from the first mention of that kind of idea way back in Genesis when Cain killed his brother. God asked him what he had done, and he said nothing. Then God said, "What have you done? Listen! Your brother's blood cries out to Me from the ground" (Gen. 4:10). We come to Jesus, the mediator of a new covenant and the sprinkled blood that speaks a better word than the blood of Abel (Heb. 12:24), for Abel's blood, along with all the martyrs under the altar, is saying, "How long until You take vengeance?" but the blood of Jesus is saying, "Forgive. Reconcile. Redeem."

Charles Wesley wrote a great hymn about this, speaking of Jesus presenting His blood in the presence of the Father:

> *Five bleeding wounds He bears,*
> *Received at Calvary.*
> *They pour effectual prayers,*
> *They strongly plead for me.*
> *Forgive, forgive I hear them cry,*
> *Nor let that ransomed sinner die.*

(from "Arise My Soul")

There is blood that speaks in the presence. There is the blood of the Lamb that says "forgive." But there is blood that speaks in the presence that says, "Lord, judge," and the two are not contradictory. God wants all men to be redeemed, but God will not overlook the wicked, because He is the God of justice and of mercy. We have looked at Habakkuk, a very important Scripture: "In wrath remember mercy" (Hab. 3:2). Both things come together in God. The great thing for us in all the persecutions that come is that they might kill us, but they cannot shut us up—our blood will continue to speak: "By faith he still speaks, even though he is dead" (Heb. 11:4).

Just and True Judgments

The sixth angel sounded his trumpet, and I heard a voice coming from the horns of the golden altar that is before God. It said to the sixth angel who had the trumpet, "Release the four angels who are bound at the great river Euphrates." And the four angels who had been kept ready for this very hour and day and month and year were released to kill a third of mankind. The number of the mounted troops was two hundred million. I heard their number. The horses and riders I saw in my vision looked like this: Their breastplates were fiery red, dark blue, and yellow as sulfur. The heads of the horses resembled the heads of lions, and out of their mouths came fire, smoke and sulfur. A third of mankind was killed by the three plagues of fire, smoke and sulfur that came out of their mouths. The power of the horses was in their mouths and in their tails; for their tails were like snakes, having heads with which they inflict injury (Revelation 9:13-19).

Although I have said that God moves in measurements of quality rather than in lines of quantity, God always moves at exactly the right moment. It is when the fullness of time had come that God sent His Son into the world (Gal. 4:4). The Bible also tells us when Jesus will come again. It says, "At the right moment." He will always come at precisely the right moment, and now we see the exactness of God as He releases judgments through angels who had been kept for this very hour, day, month, and year. When God moves, it is always the right time. And notice that it is the altar that calls upon God to release His judgments into the world. We have another recapitulation here. Remember back in chapter 7 that the angel held back the four winds until there was a seal on the foreheads of the believers. Now, probably relating to the same moment, the worshipers in Heaven are saying to God, "Release the angels now. The time for judgment has come." We as the people of God and those who have gone before us into the presence of God are those who work with God to call His judgments down into our world.

There were two hundred million demon forces released into the world. If we look at them, we can discover at least something about them. They are horses and riders again. Horses and riders, we have already seen, in some places represent the angel messengers of God. These in chapter 9 are clearly violent and foul, and they have upon themselves the very marks of hell. We know this because later on in the Book of Revelation we are going to encounter a lake of burning sulfur and where there is burning sulfur, there is the glowing red of flame, the deep blue of smoke and the bright yellow of sulfur itself. So, these mounted troops have the color of hell upon them. They smell of the lake of fire. God has released hell on Earth. Not for you and me though, because we have the seal of God upon us. Their breastplates are fiery red, like the flames of the lake, dark blue, like the smoke that rises from it forever, and sulfur yellow, like the stench of that which burns in order to consume all the enemies of God. What is more, out of their mouths comes fire, smoke, and sulfur. So, what covers their heart comes out of their mouth. The breastplate is that which covers the heart. It is fiery red, dark blue, and sulfur yellow. Therefore, it should not surprise us that flames and smoke and sulfur come out of their mouths, for out of the fullness of the heart the mouth speaks. That is not only true of the saints who fill their hearts with the Word of God. That is true of evil men.

The evil man brings forth the evil things out of his heart. Now we are confronted with a multitude whose hearts are corrupt, and therefore out of their mouths comes all kinds of evil. The evil that comes out of their mouth is turned into a plague, as it affects and touches and influences the world upon which they come. The words that come out of mouths can be the most harmful weapons that you and I ever encounter. When we were children and other children bullied or made fun of us on the playground, we would say, "Sticks and stones can break my bones, but names will never hurt me." But we have grown up to understand that name-calling can do more lasting damage than any stick or stone. These evil men come out spewing fire and breathing smoke; they have got the worst smelling breath ever encountered! It stinks like rotten eggs as they spew out their sulfurous horror.

Now remember that the altar has called all this forth. Why? So that men, in their hurt, in their despair, in their agony, might find solace with the Lord. Just as Jesus calls Himself the first and the last, the beginning and the end, so these warriors have death first and last, beginning and end. The horses have mouths like lions to devour and tails like snakes to torment. The very beginning of them and the end of them is all about death, just as the beginning and the end of Jesus is all about life. Let me refer you to one more Scripture:

> *The third angel poured out his bowl on the rivers and springs of water, and they became blood. Then I heard the angel in charge of the waters say:*
>
>> *You are just in these judgments,*
>> *You who are and who were, the Holy One,*
>> *because You have so judged;*
>> *for they have shed the blood of Your saints*
>> *and prophets,*
>> *and You have given them blood to drink as they deserve.*
>
> *And I heard the altar respond: "Yes, Lord God Almighty, true and just are Your judgments"* (Revelation 16:4-7).

Isaiah had said, "When Your judgments come upon the earth, the people of the world learn righteousness" (Isa. 26:9)—but sometimes not as swiftly as they should. Such is the case here. They continued to be unrepentant of their wicked deeds and demon worship (see Rev. 9:20-21).

Brothers and sisters, we must be convinced that true and just are His judgments. When God came down to destroy the cities of the plain, when He came down to cast burning sulfur on Sodom and Gomorrah, when He came to turn them into an unquenchable fiery furnace, Abram stood before Him and said, "But what if there are some righteous?" God replied, "If there are a few righteous I will spare the city." Here, of course, was the tragedy: none were righteous. But Abraham took his unwavering faith stance on this truth: "Will not the Judge of all the earth do right?" (Gen. 18:23-25). This is our confidence. This is our security. Whatever God unleashes, the Judge of all the earth will always do right.

CHAPTER 10

The Angel of the Covenant

The prophet Malachi was a "preparer of the way." He was the man who closed the chapter on Old Covenant revelation. One of the great promises he makes is this:

> *"See, I will send My messenger, who will prepare the way before Me. Then suddenly the Lord you are seeking will come to His temple; the messenger of the covenant, whom you desire, will come," says the Lord Almighty* (Malachi 3:1).

The word messenger is exactly the same word as angel. That is what an angel is: he is a messenger from God. Our subject for this chapter is "the angel of the Covenant" or "the messenger of the Covenant," the one who comes to reveal the purposes of God in all their fullness.

Then I saw another mighty angel coming down from heaven. He was robed in a cloud, with a rainbow above his head; his face was like the sun, and his legs were like fiery pillars. He was holding a little scroll, which lay open in his hand. He planted his right foot on the sea and his left foot on the land, and he gave a loud shout like the roar of a lion. When he shouted, the voices of the seven thunders spoke. And when the seven thunders spoke, I was about to write; but I heard a voice from heaven say, "Seal up what the seven thunders have said and do not write it down." Then the angel I had seen standing on the sea and on the land raised his right hand to heaven. And he swore by Him who lives for ever and ever, who created the Heavens and all that is in them, the earth and all that is in it, and the sea and all that is in it, and said, "There will be no more delay! But in the days when the seventh angel is about to sound his trumpet, the mystery of God will be accomplished, just as He announced to his servants the prophets." Then the voice that I had heard from heaven spoke to me once more: "Go, take the scroll that lies open in the hand of the angel who is standing on the sea and on the land." So I went to the angel and asked him to give me the little scroll. He said to me, "Take it and eat it. It will turn your stomach sour, but in your mouth it will be as sweet as honey." I took the little scroll from the angel's hand and ate it. It tasted as sweet as honey in my mouth, but when I had eaten it, my stomach turned sour. Then I was told, "You must prophesy again about many peoples, nations, languages and kings" (Revelation 10:1-11).

The angel of God came down and found John on the Island of Patmos. As we read the description of this angel, as we see another awesome representation of a heavenly being, we are pressed to the conclusion that this angel is none other than Jesus Himself. It should not surprise us that we are talking about Jesus as an Angel. It should not disturb us theologically to see Jesus in this way because that is how we meet Him all the time in the Old Testament. Every pre-incarnate appearance of Christ in the Old Testament has Him described as the "Angel of the Lord" or the "Angel of His Presence." Not only that, but this Angel of the Lord speaks as if He Himself is God. He receives worship and gives commands. He is none other than the Lord Himself. It was the Angel of the Lord that appeared in the bush and who spoke to Moses. This is another enigma, demonstrations of the pre-incarnate Christ in all His divinity, taking on Angelic form to communicate to mankind. He is the ultimate messenger, God's last Word. There is no greater message than the message that Jesus brings. There is no greater revelation than the revelation that Jesus speaks into our hearts. The Angel of the Lord has come. Jesus has appeared.

The Cloud and the Covenants

There are tremendous similarities between this Angel and the risen Christ that we saw in Chapter 1, a striking family re-semblance. If this is not Jesus, it must be His twin brother. They both have a face that shines like the sun. Both of them stand on fiery legs and, what is more, this Angel, who comes down out of Heaven, is robed in a cloud, and in the Scriptures the only one who robes himself in the dark clouds of the sky is God. If this is not God, he has stolen God's coat! He has come down dressed in a cloud because clouds in the Scripture always represent the presence of God. God makes Himself known in the cloud. God speaks out of the cloud. He is enthroned in the cloud above the cherubim. He communicates to His people in the cloud. He came down the mountain in a cloud. God dwells in clouds. When Jesus is on the mountain of transfiguration and His face starts shining like the sun, even in His earthly body, then a great cloud surrounds Him. He is not only shining like the sun, He is robed in a cloud out of which God speaks. When Jesus ascended back into the presence of the Father, He went up in a cloud, and when He comes again, He is coming in the clouds. And here is Jesus with His visitation coat on. He is dressed in a cloud. We are encountering Christ again in this Angelic manifestation.

He also represents, in His stance, in His appearance, in His attitudes, all the covenants that God has made with humanity down through the years since the beginning of time. As we have seen, there are those that teach that the Bible is structured around dispensations. There is disagreement between dispensationalists about how many dispensations there are, but there are several. The calamity, as you look at such a doctrine and such a structure, is this: all of them end in disaster. All of them end in failure, and the ultimate one for them, which is the Church Age, also ends in failure because it climaxes with the Laodicean church. That is when Jesus comes and rescues us from our imminent failure, rescues us from our inevitable decline, and accomplishes worldwide salvation when we are out of the way.

It is not arrogance and self-interest that makes me dissatisfied with such a proposition. It is because I find that all the way through Scripture God never invested in failure. The God who begins something is the God who completes it. God does not entertain the thought that what He has embarked upon could come to ruin. God begins well and ends up better. The purposes of

God unfold with greater and greater glory. Rather than seeing the Bible structured around a number of dispensations, you can see clearly when you read the Scriptures that everything is built around covenants.

God is the God of covenants, and God has never related to man outside of a covenant. God has made it very clear that He has rules of engagement with His people. There are many covenants, and covenant was a recognized way of nations relating together in these distant and biblical times. There would be clearly defined parameters of behavior and expectation between two people who entered into covenant. Some meet around a board to discuss, others go to arbitration to beat out the details, but God does not make covenant like that. When God made a covenant, it was a covenant between a Sovereign and His servants. There was no question of equality. There was no sitting around and thrashing out the details. There was no going to arbitration. God would say, "These are the terms of the covenant. You can receive them, you can reject them, but you cannot change them. They are not open to negotiation. This is My covenant. It carries great demands but innumerable blessings."

There is a little word or sentence that recurs through the Scriptures from the beginnings in Genesis right through to the Book of Revelation that some teachers have said encapsulates the concept of covenant. It goes like this: "I will be your God and you will be My people." That encapsulates the covenant relationship into which we have come with the Lord. "I will be your God." That contains a demand, and it has a benefit. It demands that I worship Him. It demands that I put Him in first place. It demands that He have all of my life. But it also means that if He is my God, He will meet all my needs. If He is my

God, He will never leave me nor forsake me. If He is my God, He will lead me in paths of righteousness and make me lie down in green pastures. If He is my God, this covenant entails great responsibility, but it also brings me immense benefit and blessing.

"You will be My people." The emphasis is on belonging; there is a sense of ownership. You are not your own; you have been bought with a price. In the Book of Revelation the first mention of the blood of Jesus in chapter 1 says that He "has freed us from our sins by His blood" (Rev. 1:5). There is liberty. There is a release. But when they sing one of the songs in Revelation, they sing, "And with Your blood You purchased men for God" (Rev. 5:9). Our redemption is not just freedom from sin; it has freed us from sin and purchased us for God. I now have new ownership and a new Master.

All Things Under His Feet

God is a covenant-keeping God, and down through history God has made covenants with His people. As we look at the Angel, it seems to me that He deliberately embodies the covenants of God that have been made in Scripture. For instance, when He comes down, He is a gigantic Angel. Firstly, He is huge because it appears that He straddles continents. He comes and puts one foot on the land and one foot on the sea in a dramatic pose that declares without a word this great truth: "All things are under My feet." Later on, in chapter 13, we are going to see a beast coming out of the ocean and a beast coming out of the land. It is good to know that before either of them even raises their ugly heads, they are already under the feet of the Lord Jesus Christ! But this is a pose of the very covenant with which God began His purposes in our world. When He created a man in His image, He said, "Be fruitful, multiply, fill the earth, subdue it and rule over all the works of My hands." David, when he walks out one night and gazes skywards, becomes amazingly aware of his own frailty and insignificance within the vastness of God's creation. He says:

> *When I consider Your heavens, the work of Your fingers, the moon and the stars, which You have set in place, what is man that You are mindful of him, the son of man that You care for him? You made him a little lower than the heavenly beings and crowned him with glory and honor. You made him ruler over the works of Your hands; You put everything under his feet* (Psalm 8:3-6).

David is recalling that first covenant relationship into which God moved with the man He had created and said, "Under your feet will be all things." When the writer of the Hebrews is speaking of what God has planned and purposed for man, he quotes this Psalm. What I like about him is that he quotes it but cannot remember where the Scripture is. That is very encouraging for some of us, who always have a problem with books, let alone chapters and verses. The writer of the Hebrews says, "Someone, somewhere said." Hallelujah, a fellow traveler! Then he says, "Yet at present we do not see everything subject to him" (Heb. 2:8). Now let me emphasize something here. He is not talking about Jesus; he is talking about man. He asks, "What is man?" God has not given angels the rule of the world to come, but men. And so he says, "What is man that You are mindful of him?" But at the moment we do not see all things under his feet, but we do see Jesus crowned with glory and honor. Why do we need to see Jesus? Because all things are under His feet. If you cannot see all things under the feet of Jesus, whose feet are they under? Not everything knows it is under the feet of Jesus, but that is where it is. In Ephesians, Paul tells us, "God has put all things under His feet" and, because they are under His feet, God's intended will and purpose is that all things come under our feet. "All things" coming under our feet is demonstrated in how we confront and overcome the evil one. We bring him under our feet by crushing his head. We will look at more of that later, but this is the covenant that God made. This is a pose that demonstrates and speaks of the greatness of God who has put everything under the feet of Jesus.

A Covenant With Creation

Next we can note that above the head of this Angel is a rainbow. We know that the rainbow is God's sign of His covenant, not just with Noah and his descendants, but with all the creatures of the earth and with inanimate creation itself. There is a covenant that God has made with the fabric of our planet. When sin came into the world, it had universal repercussions. In an earlier chapter we considered the centrality of the throne, and we said that if you drop the pebble in the pool the ripples go out, and that is the picture of Jesus and the influence of His rule. But conversely that was also the effect of sin. When sin came into the world, it was like an evil stone had dropped into the beautiful pool of God's creation and set defiling ripples in motion that went to the furthest reaches of the universe. Sin did not just affect Adam. It did not just affect us as the offspring of Adam. God said, "Cursed is the ground because of you" (Gen. 3:17). And thorns and thistles are a sign of God's displeasure in a fallen world. It is an interesting study to follow the whole concept of thorns and thistles through the Scriptures. Here was a sign of a world in de-creation, a world in decay. It is not at all coincidence, nor is it for a moment just a mark of Roman cruelty, that when Jesus died they wove a crown of thorns and wedged it on His head. It was a dramatic demonstration that Jesus was not just taking your sin; He was carrying away the curse that is on the universe. That is why the whole creation is groaning, travailing up until now. It is looking to be released from its bondage to corruption. If we had ears tuned to hear it, the trees are groaning, the grass is crying, the desert is moaning. Why? Because they are waiting to be released from the corruption that came upon them because of sin. We look forward to a world restored and redeemed. You see the blood that was shed on the cross did not just bring us near to God. Paul writes to the Colossians and says,

> *For God was pleased to have all His fullness dwell in Him, and through Him to reconcile to himself all things, whether things on Earth or things in Heaven, by making peace through His blood, shed on the cross* (Colossians 1:19-20).

I don't fully know what that means. I don't know what the full implications of that are. I just know that if there is anything in the vastness of God's creation that has been spoiled by sin, that has been moved out of harmony because of corruption, then the blood of Jesus is both sufficient and efficient to bring everything back into right relationship to Him. The rainbow says, "I am going to bring all things back into harmony. I have a covenant with inanimate creation. I have a covenant with the birds and the beasts. I have made a covenant with mankind and I will make all things new."

A Covenant of Promise

The Angel of the Covenant stands then, and He raises His hand to Heaven and swears by Him who lives forever and ever that there will be no more delay. Note that this is the very posture that God adopts in Deuteronomy: "I lift My hand to heaven and declare: As surely as I live forever" (Deut. 32:40); interestingly, it is also the stance of Abraham himself when he made an oath to God: "I have raised my hand to the Lord, God Most High, Creator of heaven and earth, and have taken an oath" (Gen. 14:22). This stance that He takes, the stance that Jesus adopts, is the same stance in many ways that He adopted when He made a covenant with Abraham:

> *When God made His promise to Abraham, since there was no one greater for Him to swear by, He swore by himself, saying, "I will surely bless you and give you many descendants." And so after waiting patiently, Abraham received what was promised* (Hebrews 6:13-15).

And now the Angel stands in that same covenantal stance, and He swears by Him who lives forever and ever. He is swearing by Himself. There is no one greater for Him to swear by. And He promised, just as He promised Abraham, that there would be an heir, and Abraham waited patiently for the fulfillment. Now the Angel raises His hand to Heaven and swears by God that there will be no more delay, that the promise is about to be fulfilled, that the expectation is about to be met, that joy will break out on those who for many long years have waited to see the visitation of God. He takes a covenant pose, and He speaks into the Heavens and makes a promise to the world.

Led Into Covenant Blessing

He stands on two fiery pillars for legs. As soon as we see those fiery pillars, we cannot help but remember that is how He appeared to Israel in the wilderness. That is how He led Moses into covenant relationship. God walked before His people by night as a fiery pillar and by day as a column of smoke, the two great legs of God marching through the wilderness. Remember those other Scriptures that we thought about in Judges and Psalm 68, when God marched before His people through the wasteland: it was on two great legs of smoke and fire. He led them on two great legs visible in their glory that men had to follow and pursue to be safe and secure. The Angel comes down now with fiery pillars for legs, and He is saying, "I am going to lead you into all the blessings of God. I am going to lead you into the entire covenant that God has made for you. I am going to take you into the fulfilling of God's promise and all the blessings of the Lamb. Just follow Me. I am going to walk on covenant legs so bright and so shiny and so glorious that even in the darkest night you will see them. You will see and follow Me into all the blessings that I have ordained for you."

The Covenant and the Kingdom

One of the wonderful aspects of this Angel—and it is an aspect that we have met before with the Christ who manifests Himself to John on the Island of Patmos—is that His face shone like the sun. That is a wonderful picture of the covenant of kingship. There are five great covenants that God made in the Old Testament: the covenant with Adam, the covenant with Noah, the covenant with Abraham, the covenant with Moses, and the covenant with David. God's covenant with David was that they would never lack one to sit on his throne, for God wanted His people to be a ruled and a governed people. It is only those who are under authority who can exercise authority. This is the key to Kingdom living. This you remember from when the centurion came to Jesus and surprised Him with his faith. The covenants are not unrelated; they are actually progressive.

Adam

The covenant that God first made with Adam sets the pattern for everything that God wants to do from that moment on. I teach students at a Bible school on the subject "What the Bible Is All About." I have sought to show them that in the opening chapters of Genesis you understand everything that God wants to do. The rest of the Bible is just working out the purpose of God. Right at the beginning we understand what God wants to do. He wants to fill the earth with people like Himself. That was His mandate to Adam. He wants to fill the earth with people like Himself, a people who will exercise authority and custodianship over creation and not only be confined to the garden; He wants the garden to become a garden without boundaries, to fill the earth just as the four rivers flowed to the four corners of the earth. That was God's plan. Adam sinned, but that did not mean that God had failed, nor did it mean that satan now took the authority. Later on the Psalmist can still say, "The earth is the Lord's, and everything in it, the world, and all who live in it" (Ps. 24:1). It is still God's world.

Noah

When God made His covenant with Noah it was a reaffirmation of His plan and His purpose. It is very interesting that when Noah's father named him, he named him in light of the curse that was on the ground because of Adam's sin. It says, "He named him Noah and said, 'He will comfort us in the labor and painful toil of our hands caused by the ground the Lord has cursed'" (Gen. 5:29). So they saw the coming of Noah as giving them rest from the curse, no longer struggling, no longer striving, but resting in the grace and the goodness of God. Just as God had brought all the animals to Adam that he might name them, He brings all the animals to Noah that he might save them. When Noah comes out of the Ark, he literally and spiritually comes into a new Heaven and a new Earth. The flood has changed the whole of the Earth. This was not a little localized downpour. This was a cataclysmic, world-wide disaster. Everybody on Earth was removed, all the mountains were destroyed, and geography itself would have been altered because not only did the rains fall down but also the fountains of the deep were opened. There would have been earthquakes and volcanoes that totally disrupted the world as they knew it, and when he came out of the Ark, it was into a new world, a new Earth. What is more, he lived under new heavens because, before the flood, there was a firmament, like a great vapor that surrounded the earth and kept the climate constant and manageable, probably filtered out all the ultraviolet rays that caused aging, enabling people to live much longer. But now that was gone.

It had all fallen down onto our earth. So he literally comes out into a new Heavens and a new Earth. What is more, there is a new sign in the Heavens that had never been there before. There is a rainbow in a new Heavens and a new Earth. He comes out to be God's new Adam and receives the same commission. God says, "It does not matter who fails, it does not matter how many times they fail. My purpose and My plans will be fulfilled."

Abraham

Then God makes His covenant with Abraham because it is in Abraham that all the families of the earth will be blessed. It is in Abraham that God wants to release not just men and women who have been delivered from darkness, not just men and women who have been rescued from the curse, but men and women who know the blessing of God in their lives, that blessing that makes rich and adds no sorrow to it (Prov. 10:22). In his seed all the families of the earth were to be blessed. There is a worldwide redemption set in motion through the faith of our father Abraham. It is through the seed of this one man.

Moses

When God makes a covenant with Moses, it is that He might have a people, a nation, who will demonstrate His goodness, walk in His ways, obey His Word, do His will, and, in doing it, get so blessed that they will be a provocation to all the nations around them. It is not at all coincidental that He established them on the land bridge that joins three continents, because God wanted them in the middle of the world so that all men could see and be provoked to jealousy. That is why Jesus speaks of the Queen of Sheba, who came to see the wisdom of Solomon. She only came from down the road, but Jesus says she came from the ends of the earth. That is what was supposed to happen. The ends of the earth were supposed to come and seek the Lord.

David

For God's people, a nation that was God's nation and a community that would be ruled by God's King, God chose David. The sun speaks of the rule and government of King David. Here is God's promised covenant to David:

> *His line will continue forever and his throne endure before Me like the sun* (Psalm 89:36).

His throne is going to be like the sun. His government will be like the sunshine. David's own testimony of God's dealings with him in life is recorded in these terms:

The God of Israel spoke, the Rock of Israel said to me:
"When one rules over men in righteousness, when he rules
in the fear of God, he is like the light of morning at sunrise
on a cloudless morning, like the brightness after rain that
brings the grass from the earth" (2 Samuel 23:3-4).

God told David what it was like to be a good king. What is it
like to be a good king? What is it like to rule in righteousness?
It is like the light of day at sunrise. The sun represents the
Kingdom. When Jesus told parables of the Kingdom, with the
removal of everything that defiles and the taking away of
everything that spoils, He said, "Then the righteous will shine
like the sun in the Kingdom of their Father" (Matt. 13:43).
God's Kingdom is a sunshine Kingdom because the King has
a sunshine face. The sunshine face of Jesus, I believe, portrays
for us very graphically the kingdom covenant that God made
with David. Right from the beginning, before there was a man
that ever walked on the earth, the sun shone as a sign of God's
government. God made a great light to govern the day, and so
the sun in the sky was a picture and a communication of God's
Kingdom.

This world was not random. It was not a mistake. It did not
happen by accident. Ours is a governed world. Ours is an ordered
world. It is a world where things happen in almost predictable
ways because God is a consistent King and a conscientious
Ruler. We have no room for the idea that God is the celestial
clockmaker who wound it up and then departed and leaves it
going until it runs down. God upholds all things by the word of
His power. He is still intimately involved in our world, and He
has set signs in the skies. Everything in our world speaks to us
about God. That is its prime purpose. Creation speaks to us of

God. Paul says that the things that are made clearly portray to us the invisible attributes of God. There is a visible and a vocal testimony of God in our world. We are without excuse if we neglect God. We are without excuse if we reject God. We are without excuse if we do not believe in God, for the evidence is on every hand, and the testimony rings out day after day, night after night, for the glory of God is seen and heard in all that He has made. Or in the words of the psalmist, "The heavens declare the glory of God; the skies proclaim the work of His hands" (Ps. 19:1).

No Longer Strangers

The Angel of chapter 10 is dressed and positioned to communicate all of the past covenants that God has made. Now you might ask, how does it affect me? When Paul is writing to the Ephesian church, he is speaking to people who were Gentiles by ethnic origin. Because they were Gentiles, Paul says they were "strangers to the covenants of promise." But he continues: "Now in Christ Jesus you who once were far away have been brought near through the blood of Christ" (Eph. 2:13). There are two important things here. First of all, all the covenants that God made down through history were covenants of promise. That is, they all looked forward to a fulfillment. All the covenants, actually, were facets and shadows of the ultimate covenant that was yet to come. So each of them promised something. Paul says this: once we were strangers to the covenants, but now in Christ we are no longer strangers. Therefore, every one of the covenants must be relevant to us. Every covenant finds its fullness in Jesus. That is why this Angel is Jesus. He is the messenger of the covenant who has suddenly come to His temple. He has arrived and is demonstrating all the promises of God through history because, however many promises God has made, however vast

190

they are, however multitudinous, they are yes and amen in Christ (2 Cor. 1:20)! Do you know there is no promise outside of Christ? There is no promise of salvation outside of Christ. There is no promise of being useful to the Master outside of Christ. There is no hope for Israel outside of Christ. All the promises are yes and amen in Him. He stands as the great Angel of the Covenant. It is into this great covenant that we have come. For God sent Christ to be a covenant for the people (Isa. 49:8), and in Christ we are called to subdue our world. We look forward to new Heavens and a new Earth. It is through the Church that all the families of the earth will be blessed, for we now constitute God's holy nation of priests, and we are the citizens of the Kingdom that is destined to fill the earth.

No Longer Observing

There are further things that relate this Angel to Jesus. In chapter 5, a mighty Angel comes down from Heaven and says, "Who is worthy?" Now this chapter begins, "And I saw another mighty Angel." So immediately he is relating us back to chapter 5. The one whom he saw worthy to open the scroll was the Lion of the Tribe of Judah. Now this Angel comes down and cries with a voice like a lion. He takes the scroll, He opens all the seals and looses the purposes of God. He has set into motion all that God wants to do. Someone will say, "But this one specifically says it is a little scroll." It looks like a little scroll because He is such a big Angel!

Up until now John had been taking notes. John has been writing, recording everything. Everything at this moment is going to change. He is not going to write, he is going to eat. He is going to take the scroll and eat the scroll and fill himself with the scroll. It is important for us that we do not just note the

Word, give mental assent to the Word, or think about the Word, but that we devour the Word, eat the Word, that we fill our hearts and our lives with the Word of God. John is going to pass from being an observer to being a participator in all that is going on. Something is going to change. John's ministry up until now has been to be a recorder; now he is going to be a worker in the purpose of God. And when we look into the next chapters, we are going to find that is exactly what he is going to do. The Angel tells him, "You need to eat this book because you are going to prophesy again" and then we move into chapters all about God's prophetic people.

God does not want to inform us. He wants us to be filled with the word that will change us, that will equip us, and that will enable us to take the message of the Kingdom to the ends of the earth. And the Angel of God, the Angel of the Covenant, stands in our midst with a book open in His hands and He says, "Get that inside you and see what will happen!"

Concluding Remarks

Let me first bring a conclusion to the last chapter regarding this Angel of the Covenant. He gives John the scroll to eat, and in many ways it is a reenactment of what happened to Ezekiel at the beginning of his ministry, where he is given a scroll not by an angel but by the Son of Man, who is seated upon the throne, again a strong indication that this Angel is our Lord Jesus Christ. He gives him the open scroll, and upon the scroll are written calamities and woes. He eats the scroll, and in eating it he finds that it is sweet to taste. We will always have that enigma and that dilemma if we are to be the true servants of God. To us the Word will always be sweetness. It will always be a delight. But to those who hear it from us, it will sometimes be bitter. It will sometimes be difficult. And so we identify in some ways with those to whom we have to take the Word. Every word of God has two sides: blessing or curse, life or death. And to some of those to whom we speak it, it will be the Word of life, but to others it will be the word of death. So, although we delight in the Word ourselves, we understand that to many it will be bitterness and therefore, in a measure, we identify with their bitterness. We feel the burden and the responsibility of those who carry the Word of God. Jeremiah was, of course, a man who had, one could almost say, a failed ministry. He was faithful to God, but he did not see people turn to the Lord. He did not see the acceptance of his word, although he preached it in obedience to God and he preached it with the anointing of the Spirit. But people did not respond. Those he addressed were not those who would listen and take to heart the Word of God from His mouth:

> *When Your words came, I ate them; they were my joy and my heart's delight, for I bear Your name, O Lord God Almighty* (Jeremiah 15:16).

This is an expression of Jeremiah in his relationship with the Word. But we cannot just have relationship with the Word; we have to have relationship with the Word *and the world.* It would be nice to be cloistered away, secreted somewhere in some monastery, and just give ourselves to the Word. But God wants to give us to the world. The Word that is in us brings life to the world or, conversely, death to the world. So Jeremiah gets to that place where he says, "I am tired of this. I'm not sure if I can cope with this anymore. I don't know if I can stand another rejection. I don't think I will speak in His name anymore." He comes to that place and he says, "There is a fire in my bones that I cannot quench and I have to speak." There is the delight, but there is a struggle that goes on inside. This Word is not just for you and your devotions or your personal inspiration or your growth in God. The Word is given to you that you might give the Word to the world, and the world is not going to delight in it in the same way you do; therefore, it is sweetness but bitterness, too. The Word of God is always a sweet thing, sweeter than honey from the honeycomb the psalmist said. It has bitter repercussions at times, but we must be a people who delight ourselves in the Word of God and fill ourselves with it. We too must eat the scroll as John did, for it is the "the Word planted in you" (James 1:21) that produces salvation; it is the Word of God that "lives in you" (1 John 2:14), that makes you strong and causes you to overcome.

CONTACT THE AUTHOR

Tony Ling
www.schooloftheprophets.co.uk
info@schooloftheprophets.co.uk

School of the Prophets
Station Road
Stoney Stanton
Leics, LE9 4LU, UK

PROPHETIC ENGAGEMENT,
THE ISSACHAR MANDATE

*Unlocking the Hidden Power of the
Interpretive Function in the Gift of Prophecy*

By Obii-Pax-Harry

And this Gospel of the Kingdom shall be preached in all the world for a witness unto all nations; and then shall the end come (Matthew 24:14).

Now is the time to reach out and share God with the world. Using the gifts He gave you will bring about His purpose in your life—and the Church as a whole.

Prophetic Engagement is a "clarion call" to the prophetic church to:

* Reposition the gift of prophecy to an interpretative role.
* Engage more proactively with Christian media.
* Serve the unsaved world with divine abilities granted by God.
* Establish an apostolic and prophetic Christian media army.
* Set firm foundations so the house of God can stand as designed.

Learn today how you can move the Gospel forward!

ISBN:88-89127-31-7

BOOKS TO HELP YOU GROW STRONG IN JESUS

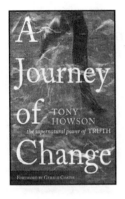

A JOURNEY OF CHANGE

The Supernatural Power of Truth

By Tony Howson

When is Truth not The Truth?

Experiencing the Spirit of Truth opens your life to incredible fullness in God. Allowing the Spirit of Truth to guide your life and influence your decisions will lead you into an exciting new realm of joy and purpose.

"And you shall know the truth, and the truth shall set you free" (John 8:32).

Learn the difference between:

Truth and Holy Spirit Truth.
A then experience and a now experience.
Saul and Paul.
A suddenly and a dead tradition.
Right and wrong.

Experience the Spirit of Truth today—and everyday—through your personal Comforter, the Holy Spirit.

ISBN: 88-89127-33-3

Order Now from Destiny Image Europe
Telephone: +39 085 4716623 - Fax +39 085 4716622
E-mail: ordini@eurodestinyimage.com

Internet: www.eurodestinyimage.com

Additional copies of this book and other book
titles from DESTINY IMAGE EUROPE
are available at your local bookstore.

We are adding new titles every month!

To view our complete catalog on-line, visit us at:
www.eurodestinyimage.com

Send a request for a catalog to:

**Via Acquacorrente, 6
65123 - Pescara - ITALY
Tel. +39 085 4716623 - Fax +39 085 4716622**

"Changing the world, one book at a time."

Are you an author?

Do you have a "today" God-given message?

CONTACT US

We will be happy to review your
manuscript for a possible publishing:

publisher@eurodestinyimage.com